W9-BMU-079

THE CAKEBREAD CELLARS
AMERICAN HARVEST COOKBOOK

Celebrating Wine, Food, and Friends
in the Napa Valley

THE Cakebread Cellars
AMERICAN HARVEST COOKBOOK

JACK and **DOLORES CAKEBREAD** and **BRIAN STREETER**

with Janet Fletcher

Photographs by Marshall Gordon

TEN SPEED PRESS
Berkeley

CONTENTS

INTRODUCTION

When my wife, Dolores, and I bought the property that became Cake-bread Cellars, Napa Valley was not the culinary destination it is today. The year was 1973, and if you wanted to have a nice dinner in a local restaurant then, you had better like steak.

I'm Jack Cakebread, and I'm the one who made the impulsive offer on that Rutherford cow pasture. Dolores and I were active members of the Berkeley Wine and Food Society at the time, and we enjoyed visiting Napa Valley. Besides, we wanted a new challenge. For twenty years, we had been running an auto-repair shop in Oakland—Cakebread's Garage, a business my father started. The prospect of growing and selling wine grapes and having a place in the country had a lot of appeal. When family friends offered to sell us their twenty-two acres—mostly pasture and walnut trees—Dolores and I made the leap.

The food scene in wine country was limited then, to understate the case. For years after we started Cakebread Cellars, when Dolores wanted to cook for guests, she had to bring many of the ingredients with her from Oakland. The San Francisco Bay Area's top seafood, meat, and produce purveyors did not send trucks to Napa Valley, a mere fifty miles north, because there wasn't the population or restaurant traffic to make deliveries worthwhile.

What a change we have witnessed. Today, food lovers from around the world consider Napa Valley a dining mecca. Our farmers' markets, cheese shops, wine merchants, and well-stocked grocery stores supply almost anything a serious cook could want. The surrounding region nurtures a thriving world of artisan food producers, from cheesemakers to *salumi* masters to duck farmers. And at Cakebread Cellars, we like to think that our American Harvest Workshop has helped shine a spotlight on these entrepreneurs.

EARLY LOCAVORES

We were advocates for local eating long before the word "locavore" emerged. In fact, the idea for the American Harvest Workshop—now in its twenty-fifth year—came from my feeling that American food was not getting its due. In the mid 1980s, the French and Italian governments were spending enormous sums to promote their food and wine here. Yet no one was making a similar effort to spread the word about the maturing culinary scene in America.

In 1985, I met a young Dallas hotelier who shared my thinking. Over a glass of wine, Bill Shoaf and I hatched a plan for the American Harvest Workshop, an annual retreat that would bring up-and-coming American chefs together with the best Northern California food artisans. We knew our raw materials were just as good as the products coming here from Europe. We just needed our talented chefs to recognize the quality of what was made in America and to take pride in serving it.

That first Workshop, held at the winery during the harvest of 1986, created a template for a gathering that we have now hosted for a quarter century. We have refined the itinerary over the years to keep it fresh and relevant and to incorporate new purveyors. But the Workshop's mission and the basic format have remained unchanged.

Each year, we invite five chefs from around the country to be our guests at the winery for four days in mid September to share the excitement of harvest. Call it a summer camp for chefs, if you like. Our son Dennis, who travels widely as the winery's head of sales and marketing, keeps an eye out for new restaurant talent. When he particularly enjoys a meal on the road, he'll try to get to know the chef and discern whether he or she has the kind of temperament that fits with the Workshop program.

We learned quickly that the retreat is no place for big egos. The participating chefs need to enjoy collaborating and be able to get along as a group. Over the course of the Workshop, they will plan and execute two multicourse dinners together in our winery kitchen, sharing a market basket of ingredients. We ask them to leave their signature dishes at home, to bring no ingredients with them, and to come prepared to explore and experiment with what *our* purveyors provide. It's a reality cooking show without the cameras.

In that way, the Workshop operates like a writers' or artists' colony, where like-minded people come to escape everyday pressures and to plant themselves in a new environment, in the hope of stimulating their creative juices. At the Workshop, we strive to provide a comfortable, nonjudgmental venue where chefs can take chances, share techniques, and recharge their batteries.

Initially, the Workshop was just for the trade. Although we have always invited a few journalists to participate, and in the early years we included sommeliers, the program was never open to the public. But gradually we realized that some of our "foodie" customers would enjoy being part of the experience, and in 2003 we began making a few spaces available to them. For those amateur enthusiasts (we call them Cakebread Cooks) who can secure a spot, the Workshop is a dream vacation, assisting the chefs in the kitchen, tasting wines with the company president (our son Bruce), and touring the cellar with the winemaking team.

We welcome all the participants to the winery on a Saturday afternoon with a tour of Dolores's vegetable garden and a mini farmers' market in our courtyard. Our partner purveyors are all there with samples of their products—Bellwether Farms

with its fresh ricotta and fromage blanc (page 77); Jim Reichardt with his meaty Liberty Ducks (page 147); the Hog Island Oyster folks with a raw-bar selection (page 27); and several others whom you will find profiled in the pages that follow. No transactions take place at the market; it's strictly show-and-tell and the first exposure the chefs have to the ingredients we expect them to use when the cooking gets under way.

The following three days are a whirlwind short course in winemaking, viticulture, artisan food production, and wine and food pairing. Over the years, participants have enjoyed guided chocolate tastings featuring cocoa nibs from around the world, hiked valley-floor and mountaintop vineyards with Bruce and Dennis, "cupped" coffee (that's trade talk for evaluating it) with local roasters, thrown clay with Napa Valley potters, and waded into Tomales Bay with an oyster farmer. No one becomes an expert from these experiences, but we hope all the participants gain a deeper appreciation for the effort that goes into fine wine and food.

The group spends time with our viticulturist, Toby Halkovich, learning about techniques we employ in the vineyards, such as the high-tech aerial imaging that

helps us make watering decisions. We show them some low-tech methods, too. Professional falconer Rebecca Rosen has demonstrated how she helps us protect our ripening assets in our Carneros vineyards. Birds can do a lot of damage—they know just when the grapes get sweet—so we rely on Rebecca's falcons to drive them off. We first learned about Rebecca through her work at a nearby air force base, where her falcons help keep the landing strip cleared of birds.

We also take advantage of the free labor to show Workshop participants how a harvest crew works. Early one morning, we take them to one of our vineyards, pass out grape knives, provide a brief safety lesson (those curved knives are vicious), and then divide the group into two teams. The competitive spirit prevails for about forty-five minutes as teams scurry to fill their picking bins. About the time it sinks in that grape picking is hot, sticky, backbreaking work, we call a halt, weigh the bins, and award bragging rights. Until we transitioned almost entirely to night harvesting, the *real* vineyard crew would pick alongside the chefs so the culinarians could see how fast the pros are.

Our Story in a Nutshell

DOLORES AND I MET in high school in Oakland, as World War II drew to a close. We remained sweethearts through college and married at the start of the Korean War, when I enlisted in the Air Force and didn't want to leave her unattached. By the time I finished my tour of duty, we had two sons, Steve and Dennis. Bruce, our third and final child, arrived shortly after we resettled in Oakland, in the small family home we purchased from my parents.

I went to work with my dad at his auto-repair shop, Cakebread's Garage, while Dolores looked after the boys. After my father died, I bought the garage and Dolores helped me run it. We were a team then, and we still are, sixty years into our marriage.

When we purchased the twenty-two acres in Rutherford from the Sturdivant family, we had no plans to be vintners. We thought we would grow wine grapes and sell them to others, but we were surrounded by winemakers and soon caught the bug. The University of California at Davis offered winemaking classes, and local vintners like Louis Martini and Bob Mondavi were generous with their knowledge. That foundation gave us enough confidence to make our first 157 cases, a 1973 Chardonnay from purchased grapes.

We were juggling a lot of balls in those early years. We still lived in Oakland and ran the garage, making the two-hour round trip to Napa Valley after work and on weekends. At the auto shop, we had two six-button phones, and Dolores

had to remember which one to answer with "Cakebread's Garage" and which one with "Cakebread Cellars." It seemed like we might never get to the bottom of the to-do list in Napa Valley. We had to convert the cow pasture we had purchased into a productive vineyard, equip a winery, landscape the property, and build a brand.

From the beginning, we welcomed visitors, instinctively sensing that hospitality could and should be our winery's hallmark. "Wine-and-food" has always been one word at our house, and Dolores's culinary skills blossomed with this new opportunity to entertain. She took cooking classes from some of the prominent chefs who were beginning to teach in the valley, and planted a huge vegetable garden—her first—around the winery.

To get retailers and distributors to try our wines, we would invite them to lunch or dinner. We had no kitchen at the winery then—just a grill and a microwave—but Dolores would always manage to present a nice meal, with fresh vegetables from the garden, and by the time our guests left, we had new friends and usually an order. Often we would host the staff of Bay Area restaurants that we particularly enjoyed. Many of these folks had never been to Napa Valley, and it made a big impression to visit our winery and have Dolores cook for them.

In the ensuing years, as we engaged a top architect, William Turnbull, to design our first

winery building and remodeled the farmhouse on the property, Dolores directed her attention to the grounds. She studied for and obtained certification as a Master Gardener, and she continues to oversee the ever-evolving landscape here. The colorful flower beds in front of the winery, along the highway, have become a Cakebread Cellars signature and a leading indicator of the changing seasons.

Dolores has help with the vegetable garden now—Marcy Snow is its fulltime caretaker—but she remains the last word in what we grow in this three-quarter-acre plot. We can garden year-round in Napa Valley, so our winery kitchen is always well supplied with herbs and produce from Marcy's and Dolores's efforts. When the harvest exceeds what the kitchen can use, we stock the farmstand in our parking lot and alert the winery employees. The tourists who visit us aren't usually big produce buyers—they're staying in hotels and dining out—but many of the limo drivers who bring them here are fans of our farmstand. Given the value of the vineyard land that we devote to Dolores's garden, Cakebread Cellars produce is wildly underpriced.

For our winery's two chefs, menu making begins in the garden. If Marcy has an abundance of baby turnips, Chioggia beets, and English peas, that's what they use. Many restaurants today boast about farm-to-table cooking, but it's a daily reality here, and with a much shorter distance between land and table. To have this wealth of gorgeous produce just a short stroll from the kitchen door is a chef's fantasy and perhaps why Brian Streeter has remained with us for twenty years. Brian was a twenty-two-year-old culinary school graduate when he started in our kitchen. After many years as our resident chef, he is now the culinary director and Workshop manager. Tom Sixsmith, a veteran of several of the country's top kitchens, is our day-to-day chef.

We have been hugely blessed to have two of our three sons choose to make their careers at the winery, so that Cakebread Cellars can remain in family hands. Bruce, who has a degree in viticulture and enology from the University of California at Davis, has worked at the winery since college, rising from my winemaking assistant to winemaker to company president. Dennis spent a decade in the banking industry before joining us and is now the senior vice president of marketing and sales. He is the one most likely to be on a plane to Dallas or Denver, the face of the winery to many consumers, retailers, and chefs. Steve, our oldest, works in finance and advises us on financial matters. He also travels a lot internationally and makes a point to ask for Cakebread Cellars wine wherever he dines.

After seventeen years of commuting between the winery and the auto shop, Dolores and I sold the garage in 1989. We built a home near the winery and still report for work every day, although we don't travel like we used to. For so many years, while we were building our business, we criss-crossed the country and beyond to support the chefs who were buying our wines. If they wanted Jack or Dolores Cakebread for a winemaker dinner, we were there, be it in Cincinnati, Singapore, or Tokyo. Our winery's success rests on the quality of our wines and the strength of these friendships. Now Bruce and Dennis are the winery's ambassadors and will continue our support of the culinary arts, a key objective of the American Harvest Workshop.

INTO THE CELLAR

Typically, the winery's production team is operating at full speed during the Workshop, but they always make time for a backstage tour. Either winemaker Julianne Laks or cellar master Brian Lee walks the participants through the winemaking process, starting with the buzz of activity at the crush pad, usually a frenzy of beeping forklifts and snaking hoses. Here forklift drivers may be upending the sticky contents of heavy picking bins into the press. (Watch out for bees!) Cellar workers will be pressure-washing the empty bins for the next day, cooling the air with a fine mist. In the next stop, the tank room, the winemakers explain the science of fermentation, a theoretical discussion that comes to life with samples of fresh and partially fermented juice.

From there, the tour moves to the chilly barrel room, and the talk transitions to barrel regimes: old oak or new? From which country, cooper, and forest? The permutations are many and the decisions complex. Finally, the group visits our lab and assistant winemaker Stephanie Alstott, who invites everyone to take a look through the refractometer to see how we measure a grape's sugar content. Modern wine labs like ours have a host of equipment for tracking key wine components, such as pH, tannin levels, and malic acid. Part of Stephanie's job is to monitor and interpret these rapidly changing numbers.

We hope the tour gives participants a little more context for appreciating wine. To tune their palates, we turn them over to Bruce, who guides them in a focused tasting—perhaps a vertical sampling of our Chardonnays to convey a sense of how that variety ages, or a comparative tasting of Pinot Noirs from our Anderson Valley and Carneros ranches to explore the impact of *terroir*. To complement Bruce's efforts, we import one of the country's top wine educators, Michael Weiss, a professor of wine and spirits at the Culinary Institute of America in New York. We rely on Michael to help us demystify the topic of wine and food pairing (page 18), and his lively tasting sessions with Brian Streeter, the winery's culinary director, are a Workshop highlight.

At Michael's seminars, there is always a valuable takeaway lesson. One year he served the same wine—a Cakebread Cellars Sauvignon Blanc—at three different temperatures to show how that factor affects our perception of alcohol and aroma. We hope chefs will take this awareness back to their restaurants and check that they aren't serving wines too cold (which mutes the fragrance) or too warm (which emphasizes the alcohol).

Michael and the chefs collaborate on the meals' wine selections, a process that entails a lot of give and take. A chef might have a Cabernet Sauvignon in mind for

Our Wines at a Glance

AT CAKEBREAD CELLARS, our overarching aesthetic goal is to produce wines of complexity and balance. With every variety, we want the fruit to show first, with oak in the background adding aroma and depth.

All of our white grapes are handpicked, harvested at night, and pressed as whole clusters. Manual harvesting (as opposed to machine picking) enhances quality because humans determine what ends up in the picking bins. Harvesting in the cool of the night allows us to bring grapes into the winery before the sun warms them, important to retaining their fresh flavors. And whole-cluster pressing is a gentle treatment that preserves fruit character.

SAUVIGNON BLANC

Our Sauvignon Blanc typically exhibits citrus, grapefruit, and melon aromas. The finish is crisp but never aggressively tart. We ferment some of the juice in older oak barrels to give the wine a little more depth, and we add a small proportion of Semillon for texture and Sauvignon Musqué for aroma.

CHARDONNAY

In a typical year, we barrel-ferment most of the grapes for our Chardonnay and age the wine for about eight months in about one-third new oak. In a really ripe year, we might use more tank fermentation to preserve a steely backbone. The wine shows mineral, green apple, and citrus components and has weight without being overbearing.

CHARDONNAY RESERVE

We want the Reserve wine to show more richness and complexity, so we barrel-ferment all of it and leave it in barrel for about fifteen months. Aging on the lees (the spent yeast) further enhances the wine's silky texture. It has a pronounced mineral component and surprising ageability. From a good vintage, a ten- to twelve-year old Chardonnay Reserve can offer great pleasure.

MERLOT

At Cakebread Cellars, we like to classify tannins on a spectrum from fine to firm to chalky. We expect Pinot Noir to fall on the fine end, hillside or mountain Cabernet Sauvignon on the other end, and Merlot somewhere in the middle. With our Merlot, we aim for fine-to-firm tannins and ripe berry fruit, and we add perhaps ten percent Cabernet Sauvignon for backbone.

PINOT NOIR

We grow Pinot Noir both in the Anderson Valley and in Carneros. The sites are quite different, so the wines are noticeably different, and we bottle them separately. The Anderson Valley Pinot Noir ripens later and has firmer tannins, with an attractive strawberry-raspberry component. The Carneros bottling has finer tannins and, typically, a lighter color. Both wines are macerated on the skins after fermentation to enhance the color and tannic structure.

CABERNET SAUVIGNON

We produce three or four different bottlings of Cabernet Sauvignon each year, but our objective for each is the same: we don't want the oak to overwhelm the fruit. We work hard all year to harvest top-quality grapes, and we want them to shine. For our Napa Valley bottling, we rely on fruit from several vineyard sources, from the cool Carneros region at the southern end of the valley to the warm northern end near Calistoga. This diversity of sites allows us to fashion a balanced wine with opulent fruit tempered by vibrant acidity. Depending on the vintage, we add smaller percentages of Merlot, Cabernet Franc, Malbec, and Petit Verdot for complexity. Our Benchland Select bottling comes from prime hillside vineyards in the Oakville and Rutherford appellations, including our own Hill Ranch. It has the firm structure you would expect from hillside fruit and concentrated berry aromas with warm spice notes. The Dancing Bear Ranch Cabernet Sauvignon has even deeper color, more intensity, more vigorous tannin, and higher acidity than the other bottlings. It is a focused, powerful, and persistent wine with some percentage of Merlot and Cabernet Franc added each year.

ZINFANDEL

The grapes for this wine come from a Lake County hillside vineyard planted with three clones that produce berries of different size and character. The wine shows firm tannins, aromas of ripe boysenberry and raspberry, and an intriguing dusty note.

SYRAH

This ripe, dense, dark wine comes from Carneros-grown grapes, mostly from our Suscol Springs Vineyard. We have planted some Grenache and Viognier in Carneros that we anticipate blending with this variety. In the meantime, our Syrah is a big wine suited to grilled beef and dark-meat game.

RUBAIYAT

This easygoing red wine is great fun to drink. The components change with the vintage, but we typically include small lots of Pinot Noir, Syrah, and Zinfandel. It is soft and supple, fresh and

juicy, and it ranks high on the pleasure meter. We recommend serving it cool, even lightly chilled, and consuming it young.

VIN DE PORCHE ROSÉ

Our rendition of a classic French dry rosé, Vin de Porche is intended for enjoying outdoors on casual occasions. Serve it well chilled with spicy fare or with anything prepared on the grill. A blend of Syrah and Grenache in a ratio that changes with the vintage, the wine offers fresh strawberry and cherry aromas with a subtle vanilla note and a crisp, refreshing finish.

his dish, but should it be a younger bottling or a more mature one? For an older selection, Michael might suggest adding an earthy element to the dish, such as mushrooms, to match the wine's aromatics.

Michael says that his main objective is to nurture more collaboration between a restaurant's kitchen and dining room staff. Chefs who say to their waiters, "Here's my creation. You figure out what goes with it," are depriving guests of the heightened experience that occurs when chef and sommelier collaborate.

FIELD TRIPS THAT INSPIRE

One day of the Workshop is devoted to visiting local food producers, a field trip organized by Brian, the Workshop's manager. Like winemakers, the best chefs know that they are only as good as their raw materials. That's why we treasure the relationships we have with local suppliers—the artisans who make the cheese, raise the chickens, and bake the bread that support our hospitality efforts. Some years, we load everyone into a small bus for an abbreviated tour of western Marin, a nearby county, where we can visit Point Reyes Farmstead Cheese Company, Hog Island Oyster Company, and Della Fattoria, a wood-oven bakery whose breads are prized around here. Our mission is not only to expand awareness of these top-notch producers but also to encourage Workshop chefs to find similar purveyors in their own backyards.

We plan all of these experiences—from the farmers' market to the farm tour to the wine and food pairing seminars—to inform and inspire the Workshop dinners the chefs have agreed to prepare. They will cook for seventy guests on each of two consecutive nights, performances that begin with a brainstorming session under the big oak tree on our lawn.

With Brian guiding the process, the chefs divvy up the courses and ingredients—engaging slowly at first, until someone breaks the ice. Then ideas start to fly. A chef intrigued by Don Watson's lamb proposes to grill it and serve it with chimichurri sauce. For garnish? Maybe a ragout of the 'Gypsy' peppers from Dolores's garden. Another chef speaks up for the Liberty Duck breasts. He'll pair them with pearl onions glazed with Marshall's Farm honey and a demi-glace heightened with Sparrow Lane's golden balsamic. What about braised California Vegetable Specialties endive as an accompaniment? And can you think of a wine that might work with that?

After a lot of back-and-forth and ingredient swapping—should the Bellwether Farms ricotta go in the gnocchi or in the ice cream?—the chefs have a game plan. We don't commit the menu to paper yet, but they know the general parameters of

their dishes. Around 3:00 p.m., we open the kitchen. (We don't like to let the chefs hit the stoves too soon. A little time pressure boosts the energy.)

Controlled bedlam might be the best description of what transpires over the next few hours. We have a spacious, light-filled kitchen, but it was never intended to host five chefs at once, plus photographers, consumer participants, and a handful of media. The Cakebread Cooks work alongside the chefs, getting a full immersion in the hustle and heat of the professional kitchen.

Michael Weiss floats in and out of the scene, quizzing chefs about their dishes so he can help them identify the best wine match. You're putting huckleberries in the venison sauce? Are you adding cream to that soup? Do you want an older or younger Pinot Noir with your mushroom risotto? In the weeks leading up to the Workshop, Bruce and Julianne have tasted perhaps a hundred "library wines"—the older vintages that we set aside for special occasions—to select twenty-five or thirty to showcase at the Workshop. The chefs can choose any of these selections, but they often look to Michael for guidance.

AN OCCASION FOR IMPROV

For the first five years of the Workshop, Dolores ran the show alone, but eventually she enlisted Bay Area radio personality Narsai David to help her host. Narsai had run a fine-dining establishment near Berkeley for many years, and he was Cakebread Cellars's first restaurant account, so ours is a friendship of long standing. At the Workshop, he helped the chefs orchestrate their menus—a role that Brian has since assumed—and then staked out a corner of the kitchen to make bread for dinner. Sometimes he would use fermenting grape juice for his starter. That kind of "in-the-moment" improv is what the Workshop is all about. We want chefs to seize an inspiration and run with it.

Every year, the personalities change and the group has a different chemistry. Some chefs are rowdy extroverts, others more cerebral, and the mix can get interesting. The first year, Mark Miller had everyone in the kitchen drinking margaritas, which wreaked havoc on the dinner schedule.

Dennis, who likes to cook, often lends a hand in the kitchen, hoping to pick up a tip or two. He still remembers the year he volunteered to fillet fresh sardines for San Francisco chef Mark Franz. Mark had to show him what to do, but eighty sardines later, Dennis felt like a pro.

Not surprisingly, with this many bodies in the kitchen and the clock ticking, accidents happen. Once, one of our media guests was helping a chef make pesto

Wine with Food: A Master Class

FOR MICHAEL WEISS, the educator who teaches the Workshop's wine and food pairing seminar, successful matches rely on what he calls the "tower of power." That's his evocative way of saying that the dish and the wine should be of equal intensity: lean dishes with lighter wines, richer dishes with more substantial wines.

Think of light-bodied white wines with little or no oak at the base of the tower. Pair them with delicate foods, such as lean white fish, or with simple vegetable preparations, like a spring vegetable ragout.

If you move up the tower to a white wine with more texture and oak, such as a barrel-fermented Chardonnay, you can serve a richer fish, perhaps with a butter sauce, or even a veal chop.

Climbing the tower, Pinot Noir would come next. It marries well with fattier fish, such as salmon, and with lean meats. Following Michael's "tower of power" philosophy, we sometimes serve half-portions of our Chardonnay Reserve and our Pinot Noir with the same dish. Because these varieties are close in power terms, the same dish may work with both.

Red wines with significant tannins, such as Cabernet Sauvignon, occupy the top of the power tower. They offer an opening for the fattier meats, such as well-marbled beef, short ribs, or lamb shoulder. The meat's richness can soften harsh tannins and reveal other flavors in the wine, and the tannins cut the food's richness to reveal more flavors in the dish. Isn't that what a great match is about?

Michael also helps Workshop chefs understand the flavor antagonists that can rob a dry wine of its fruit. Honey and other sweeteners, if not used judiciously, can have that impact. Highly spiced dishes paired with tannic red wine can also be less than pleasant.

Artichokes, asparagus, bell peppers, and spinach—renowned troublemakers with wine—can be tamed by the cooking method, Michael suggests. Grilling asparagus instead of steaming it, or roasting bell peppers instead of serving them raw, can make these vegetables more wine friendly.

A dish with too many components can create a sensory overload that makes a wine choice difficult. Michael sometimes has to encourage Workshop chefs to streamline their idea to make room for the wine's contribution.

and she failed to secure the lid on the blender. She turned the motor on high and an emerald-green fountain of pesto splattered all over our kitchen walls and ceiling.

Somehow, what looks like commotion in the kitchen coalesces into a beautiful and well-choreographed meal—always surprising in its flavor combinations and often awakening us to new possibilities with our wines. Although the chefs conceive and prepare their own dishes, they collaborate on the service, with the help of the Cakebread Cooks, so that seventy gleaming and garnished plates emerge from the kitchen at roughly the same time. We eat dinner on the Pecan Patio, just steps from the kitchen, so the chefs can come out and chat with our guests about their dish's evolution. I particularly remember Charlie Trotter, a Workshop participant in 1992, when it was his turn to address the diners. The shy young chef looked like he would much rather be back with his saucepans. It's a pleasure to see the self-confident restaurateur, celebrity, and role model he has become.

These two evenings on the Pecan Patio are more than just memorable dinners. They are the culmination of four days of intense camaraderie and nonstop learning, with the heady scent of the annual grape harvest in the background. The energy level in the kitchen is off the charts, thanks to the enthusiasm of the Cakebread Cooks and the fierce focus of the chefs. They are engaged in a high-wire act, after all, attempting new dishes with unfamiliar foods in a strange kitchen. Our dinner guests—an audience that often includes the featured purveyors—have the great pleasure of eating the experiments. On these balmy late-summer nights, we celebrate American culinary prowess and products and honor both with the best wines from our cellar.

You would think the chefs would be exhausted at the end of each evening, but they are just getting warmed up. Typically, they find their way to Pancha's in Yountville, where the local line cooks go for a beer after work. It's open late—rare in this valley—and the closest thing we have to a dive bar.

AND THE SHOW GOES ON

We can never predict the extent of the bonding that will take place over the course of the Workshop. You can't force it, and some years are more successful on that front than others. Certainly the most emotional corps-building experience occurred in 2001. The Workshop participants had gathered at our River Ranch vineyard early on the morning of September 11 to pick grapes. When I showed up, I saw that the doors of the pickup were open and they were all standing around it, listening to the radio.

We didn't know whether to continue with the Workshop or not, so we asked the chefs what they wanted to do. And of course, they felt the show must go on. No one could get home anyway because of the suspended flights. As it happened, one of the chefs that year was from New York City (Peter Daledda from Artisanal Fromagerie) and another from Washington, DC (Timothy Dean from Timothy Dean Restaurant), so the anxiety level was high. But staying together and working together helped us all get through that traumatic time.

Although we have tweaked the Workshop over the years, we haven't made many significant changes. One notable development is the inclusion of chefs from beyond the United States. With Cakebread Cellars expanding into global markets, and Bruce and Dennis traveling internationally, it made sense to invite some of the foreign chefs with whom we do business. In recent years, chefs from Scotland, China, India, and Japan have attended the Workshop and broadened our horizons.

When the family held that first Workshop in 1986, we could never have imagined that we would still be hosting it 25 years later. Preparations take a lot of time, but discontinuing the Workshop would leave a big hole in our lives. We maintain it in part because it reminds us why we got into the wine business in the first place— for the pride of crafting a handmade product and the pleasure of sharing it. As a result of the Workshop, we have friendships all over the country now, and beyond. Dennis boasts that he can hustle a football bet just about anywhere.

Brian and winery resident chef Tom Sixsmith benefit from the interchange with so many colleagues. Some of the visiting chefs' techniques and recipes, like Nancy Oakes's Grandmother's Soft Gingerbread Cake (page 189), become permanent parts of our repertoire. Equally rewarding are the relationships we have developed with purveyors over the years of the Workshop. Many were novice entrepreneurs just getting started and looking for markets, as we were, and it has been a pleasure to watch their businesses grow in tandem with ours.

Our family has long believed that some of the best times happen around the table. (At one memorable Workshop dinner, a young man got down on his knee and proposed. She said yes, thank goodness.) The shared experience of good wine and food has helped us forge long-lasting friendships, and the American Harvest Workshop allows us to celebrate the richness those friends bring to our lives.

In the pages that follow, you will find a collection of recipes that represent the history of the American Harvest Workshop. Some of the recipes derive from dishes that chefs created during their time here, streamlined, if necessary, to work in home kitchens. Other recipes are for dishes that former Workshop chefs are preparing today in their own restaurants. Finally, Brian and Tom have added several favorite recipes from the Cakebread Cellars kitchen to offer a seasonally balanced selection that will keep you cooking year round.

Wine from the Ground Up

THE ORIGINAL TWENTY-TWO-ACRE ranch that Dolores and I purchased in 1973 and planted to grapevines remains a key part of our vineyard portfolio. But we have added steadily to our holdings since then, acquiring choice properties in prime areas as demand for our wines grew.

We now own more than four hundred acres in Napa Valley, on eleven parcels, ranging from cool, foggy sites at the southern end of the valley, near San Pablo Bay, to a mountaintop vineyard at the valley's warm northern end. Beyond Napa Valley, we own forty-five acres in Anderson Valley, in coastal Mendocino County, a superb location for growing Pinot Noir. At the 2010 Workshop, participants started one day with breakfast in our Suscol Springs Vineyard, overlooking Carneros, and ended the day at an elevation of two thousand feet, with an *al fresco* dinner at our Dancing Bear Ranch on Howell Mountain. Virtually the entire expanse of this world-famous wine valley lies in between.

Owning this collection of properties, with their range of soil types, microclimates, and geography, gives our winemaker, Julianne Laks, maximum flexibility in the cellar. In the wines that emerge from these different parcels, she has the diversity she needs to make balanced, consistent blends, like our Napa Valley Sauvignon Blanc and Chardonnay. But she also has the potential to showcase particularly distinctive ground, as with our Dancing Bear Ranch Cabernet Sauvignon.

Each vineyard makes a strategic contribution to the mix at Cakebread Cellars. A brief overview:

DANCING BEAR RANCH

Situated on Howell Mountain, in eastern Napa Valley, this high-elevation property is well suited to warm-climate red grapes. We have Cabernet Sauvignon, Cabernet Franc, and Merlot planted in the rocky soil here and use them all in our Dancing Bear Ranch bottling. The grapes produce ripe wines with dark-fruit aromas and a characteristic forest-floor scent. The longer we work with this vineyard, the more we are convinced that those aromatic qualities are a consistent part of its signature.

MAPLE LANE VINEYARD

Near the well-known Three Palms Vineyards, on the Silverado Trail, this parcel has two distinct soil types. We grow Sauvignon Blanc in one type; Cabernet Sauvignon, Merlot, and Petit Verdot in the other. The Sauvignon Blanc ripens early and produces wine with citrus and melon aromas and a lean texture. The three reds go into our Napa Valley bottling. The Cabernet Sauvignon from Maple Lane is less hefty than our mountain-grown Cabernet, and the Merlot is especially elegant.

DOGGWOOD RANCH

This twelve-acre vineyard is on the eastern side of the valley, at about fifteen hundred feet. We have Cabernet Sauvignon and Cabernet Franc planted here, for our Napa Valley bottling. The wine made with these grapes is recognizably from hillside fruit, with firm tannins and black-cherry aromas. In some years, the two varieties ripen simultaneously and we can ferment them together, which adds complexity to the wine.

WINERY RANCHES

We own sixty-five acres around the winery, including the twenty-two-acre parcel that launched us. Some of these vines are in the Rutherford appellation, others in the Oakville appellation. The Sauvignon Blanc we grow in this area ripens early and lends a fresh grapefruit character to that bottling. We also have a little Semillon and Sauvignon Musqué on these ranches that we blend with the Sauvignon Blanc for complexity. The Cabernet Sauvignon we grow here goes into our Napa Valley bottling. It contributes a bright cherry aroma and relatively soft tannins. We have Merlot and Malbec planted here, too.

HILL RANCH

This property is in the Rutherford appellation, against the base of the western hills, with deep but well-drained soil. Planted entirely to Cabernet Sauvignon, the vineyard forms the core of our Benchlands bottling. It yields an elegant wine with a ripe black-cherry aroma and balanced tannins.

LOS CARNEROS VINEYARDS

We own four vineyards in the Carneros appellation, all in Napa County. (The appellation extends into Sonoma County as well.) These are all relatively cool sites that benefit from the moderating influence of the bay. The fog lingers in the morning and returns in late afternoon, protecting the grapes from wild temperature swings. The steady, mild temperatures are good for Chardonnay, helping the grape retain its acidity, with warm afternoons to bring the fruit to full ripeness. The soils here are ideal for white grapes.

Having these four Carneros ranches in our portfolio helps us ensure the quality of our Napa Valley Chardonnay. The properties may all be in Carneros, but they enjoy their own microclimates, so we have diversity within the appellation. The Chardonnays we make from these vineyards capture the essence of Carneros fruit: a bright green-apple and ripe pear character, without being overly tart or limey.

Our Fosters Road Vineyard, the northernmost, produces fruit for our Chardonnay and Chardonnay Reserve. We also grow a small amount of Pinot Noir here. In our Cuttings Wharf Vineyard, a little farther south, we planted Sauvignon Blanc to add complexity to our blend, balancing the qualities of the Sauvignon Blanc we grow in warmer sites. We have Chardonnay planted here, too, and it shows some potential for the Reserve program. Tinsley Ranch and Milton Road are our southernmost vineyards. The former is planted exclusively to Chardonnay; from the Milton Road parcel, we harvest Chardonnay, Merlot, and Syrah.

SUSCOL SPRINGS VINEYARD

Located on hillside slopes, this rocky vineyard has soils different from Carneros, just to the west. The area is cool, with maritime influence and minimal day-to-night temperature swings. The slopes are west facing, so the vines enjoy plentiful afternoon sun. We planted Sauvignon Blanc at the bottom of the slope; Merlot, Cabernet Franc, and Syrah in the middle; and Cabernet Sauvignon in the leanest soil at the top. We're particularly excited about the Sauvignon Blanc from this new hillside planting and expect it to add more mineral notes to our bottling.

ANDERSON VALLEY

We grow a half-dozen Pinot Noir clones, on a variety of rootstocks, on the forty-five acres we own in this Mendocino County appellation. The site's cool, foggy mornings and warm afternoons create an ideal venue for Pinot Noir. The grapes ripen fully here, yet retain their refreshing acidity.

APPETIZERS

SPRING

Hog Island Oysters with Ginger Mignonette,
Cucumber, and Wasabi Tobiko   **26**

Alsatian Tart with Leeks, Fromage Blanc, and Bacon   **29**

Tuna Tartare with Lime Crème Fraîche   **30**

Ricotta Gnocchi with Spring Herb Pesto   **31**

Michael Weiss's Gravlax   **32**

Olive Oil–Fried Egg with Roasted Asparagus and Parmesan   **34**

SUMMER

New Potatoes with Goat Cheese and Tapenade   **35**

Shrimp Corndogs with Bistro Honey Mustard   **36**

Rock Shrimp and Yuca Cakes with Spicy Mango Salad   **38**

Grilled Peaches Wrapped in Serrano Ham   **39**

Halibut *Crudo* with Shaved Radishes, Fried Capers, and Chive Oil   **40**

FALL

Kabocha Squash *Panna Cotta*   **41**

Cucumber Cups with Roasted Beets and Yogurt Dressing   **42**

Fried Green Tomatoes with Goat Cheese and Fennel Marmalade   **44**

Smoked Trout Mousse with Apple-Fennel Salad   **46**

WINTER

Warm Chopped Liver Crostini with White Truffle Oil   **47**

Thai Stone Crab Tostadas   **49**

Caramelized Onion and Walnut Biscuits with Blue Cheese Butter   **50**

Hog Island Oysters with Ginger Mignonette, Cucumber, and Wasabi Tobiko

SERVES 8

It's easy to overwhelm oysters with a topping that's too bold or too rich, but chef Rick Moonen knows just when to stop. His hors d'oeuvre, served at the 2008 Workshop, elevates the oysters' briny flavor, and frankly, it's just fun to eat. Each oyster makes a tangy splash in your mouth, with cool, warm, brisk, and sweet elements in perfect balance.

MIGNONETTE

1/4 cup unseasoned rice wine vinegar

1 1/2 teaspoons finely minced shallot

1 1/2 teaspoons finely minced fresh ginger

1/2 teaspoon sugar

1/2 teaspoon soy sauce

2 dozen Hog Island Sweetwater oysters or other fresh oysters

1/2 cup peeled and finely diced Armenian or English (hothouse) cucumber

1 ounce (about 2 tablespoons) wasabi-flavored tobiko (flying fish roe)

For the mignonette: In a small bowl, whisk together the vinegar, shallot, ginger, sugar, and soy sauce until the sugar dissolves. Cover and refrigerate for at least 2 hours.

Shuck the oysters and place them, on the half shell, on crushed ice. Top each oyster with about 1 teaspoon of the diced cucumber. Whisk the mignonette, then spoon about 1/2 teaspoon over each oyster. Top with a small spoonful of tobiko and serve immediately.

Enjoy with Cakebread Cellars Sauvignon Blanc or another white wine with lively acidity.

Oyster Madness

THE ROAD THROUGH MARIN COUNTY to Tomales Bay is twisty and a challenge for queasy types, but we like showing Workshop chefs how Hog Island Oyster Company raises its oysters and clams. As a winery renowned for its Sauvignon Blanc, we are oyster aficionados and grateful to have this sustainable shellfish farm in our "backyard."

One year, our guests climbed into boats and went out to the oyster beds for a close-up look at these bivalves growing in the cold waters of Tomales Bay—a process that takes eighteen months to three years from start to finish. The baby oysters mature in submerged net bags, feeding on phytoplankton and other nutrients that the ocean provides. Workers flip the bags occasionally to harden the shells so the edges won't be brittle.

We usually get Hog Island Sweetwaters for chefs who want to prepare oysters for a Workshop dinner. Some chefs roast small Sweetwaters in our wood oven or steam them open on the grill. Brian likes to grill them and top them with a chipotle lime butter. But every year, inevitably, one Workshop chef wants to serve raw oysters on the half shell. That's feasible in a restaurant where orders come in gradually over the course of the evening. But shucking enough oysters to serve the seventy Workshop dinner guests, who dine all at once, can send the kitchen into a temporary frenzy. One chef, who shall remain nameless, wanted to roll each raw oyster in a thin pickled cucumber strip shaved from a baby cucumber. Thank goodness there were plenty of hands on deck for that one.

Alsatian Tart with Leeks, Fromage Blanc, and Bacon

SERVES 8

Canadian chef Rob Feenie made this savory tart during the 2002 Workshop. Unlike quiche with its custard filling, the classic *tarte flambée* topping includes no egg—just fromage blanc thinned with crème fraîche, sweet sautéed onions, and smoky bacon. The name ("flaming tart") derives from earlier times, when cooks would bake it near the embers of a wood-fired oven.

1 tablespoon extra-virgin olive oil

1 onion, quartered through the root end and thinly sliced

Kosher salt

2 slices thick bacon, halved lengthwise, then sliced 1/4 inch wide

1/2 pound (or half of a 14-ounce package) frozen puff pastry, partially thawed

1/2 cup fromage blanc

2 tablespoons crème fraîche

Pinch of freshly grated nutmeg

Freshly ground black pepper

Thinly sliced fresh chives or scallions for garnish

Heat the olive oil in a skillet over medium heat. Add the onion and season with salt. Cook until softened but not colored, about 8 minutes. Let cool.

Put the bacon in a skillet over medium heat. Cook, stirring, until it renders some of its fat and just begins to crisp, about 5 minutes. Transfer it to a small bowl with a slotted spoon.

On a lightly floured surface, roll the puff pastry into a 12-inch circle (if the packaged pastry is round) or into a 10 by 12-inch rectangle (if the packaged pastry is rectangular). Transfer it to a baking sheet and prick with a fork in several places. Return it to the refrigerator for 30 minutes.

Preheat the oven to 375°F.

Put the fromage blanc, crème fraîche, and nutmeg in a small bowl and stir until smooth. Add several grinds of pepper.

Spread the fromage blanc mixture evenly over the surface of the dough, leaving a 1/2-inch bare border. Scatter the sautéed onions and bacon over the fromage blanc. Fold the border over to make a rim and crimp it as you would a pie crust. Bake until the pastry is puffed and golden-brown on the edge and well browned on the bottom, about 40 minutes. Transfer to a cutting board, sprinkle with the chives, and let cool for about 5 minutes, then cut into pieces of desired size. Serve warm.

Enjoy with Cakebread Cellars Napa Valley Chardonnay or another white wine with a full, creamy body.

Tuna Tartare with Lime Crème Fraîche

MAKES 24 (SERVES 8 TO 12)

A light, bright, citrusy hors d'oeuvre for a warm summer night, this tartare requires impeccably fresh tuna. Keep the fish on ice as you prepare it and serve it immediately for the most vivid flavor. To preserve the tuna's plum-red color, don't add the salt or soy sauce until the last moment. You can present the tartare in lettuce cups, if you prefer, instead of on fried wontons or crackers.

1/2 pound skinless sushi-grade ahi tuna

2 teaspoons extra-virgin olive oil

1/2 large jalapeño chile, seeded and finely minced

2 tablespoons finely minced red onion

2 teaspoons toasted sesame seeds

1/2 teaspoon grated lime zest

1 teaspoon soy sauce

1/4 teaspoon fleur de sel or sea salt

1/3 cup crème fraîche

1 teaspoon freshly squeezed lime juice

Kosher salt

24 fried wontons (page 49), shrimp crackers, rice crackers, or thin toasts

Finely minced scallions for garnish

Cut the tuna into neat, small dice. Place in a bowl set over ice. Stir in the olive oil, jalapeño, onion, sesame seeds, lime zest, soy sauce, and fleur de sel. In a deep bowl, whisk the *crème fraîche*, lime juice, and a pinch of kosher salt to soft peaks.

Spoon the tartare onto the fried wontons, dividing it evenly. Top each serving with a small dollop of the whipped crème fraîche and garnish with a sprinkle of scallions. Serve immediately.

Enjoy with Cakebread Cellars Sauvignon Blanc or other crisp white wine.

Ricotta Gnocchi with Spring Herb Pesto

SERVES 6

Chef Walter Pisano, a 1999 Workshop alumnus, makes an aromatic pesto that includes neither basil nor garlic. He makes it with fresh spring herbs—parsley, chives, and mint—in place of the basil that doesn't mature until summer. It's lively and light, just the right complement to his feather-light gnocchi, but you could use this pesto on fresh pasta or fish as well. Chef Pisano's gnocchi melt on the tongue when made with high-quality ricotta. At the winery, we use Bellwether Farms ricotta (see page 77), but Calabro also makes an excellent product. You may need to visit a specialty cheese shop to find fresh ricotta. Supermarket ricotta containing gums or stabilizers will not produce the most delicate gnocchi.

GNOCCHI

1 pound whole-milk ricotta

1/4 cup freshly grated Parmesan cheese

Pinch of freshly grated nutmeg

1/2 teaspoon kosher salt

Freshly ground white pepper

1/2 cup sifted all-purpose flour, or as needed

PESTO

1 cup flat-leaf parsley leaves

1/4 cup sliced fresh chives

2 tablespoons coarsely chopped fresh mint

3 tablespoons lightly toasted pine nuts

1/2 teaspoon kosher salt

1/4 cup plus 3 tablespoons extra-virgin olive oil

Freshly ground black pepper

For the gnocchi: In a large bowl, combine the ricotta, Parmesan, nutmeg, salt, and several grinds of pepper. Stir with a wooden spoon until smooth. Add just enough flour to make a soft dough that will not stick to your floured hands, about 1/2 cup. Divide the dough into four equal pieces. On a lightly floured board, with floured hands, roll each piece into a 3/4-inch-thick rope, 14 to 15 inches long, then cut each rope into 1-inch pieces. Place the gnocchi on a lightly floured tray and refrigerate for 2 hours to allow the flour to hydrate and the gluten to relax.

For the pesto: In a food processor, combine the parsley, chives, mint, pine nuts, and salt and process to a paste. With the motor running, gradually add the olive oil through the feed tube, processing until nearly smooth. Transfer to a bowl and add pepper to taste.

Bring a large pot of unsalted water to a boil over high heat. Add the gnocchi and lower the heat to maintain a bare simmer. Cook until the gnocchi float to the top, about 1 minute, then cook for 1 minute longer.

Whisk a little of the hot pasta water into the pesto to thin it to a sauce consistency. Lift the gnocchi out of the pot with a skimmer or strainer and transfer to a warmed serving bowl. Add the pesto and toss to coat evenly. Serve immediately.

Enjoy with Cakebread Cellars Napa Valley Chardonnay or another full-bodied white wine.

Michael Weiss's Gravlax

SERVES 16

A professor of wine and spirits at the Culinary Institute of America, Michael Weiss is part of our Workshop "faculty." He teaches a wine and food pairing seminar for the participants every year and selects appropriate Cakebread Cellars wines for the evening meals. That's no small challenge given how complex many of the chefs' creations are, but we give Michael carte blanche in the cellar. When entertaining at home, he and his wife, Jenny, often serve their own gravlax as a first course. In place of the fresh dill that perfumes traditional gravlax, the Weisses season the fish with coriander seed, fennel seed, and lemon. The method works beautifully on farmed Arctic char, a more sustainable choice than farmed salmon. You can serve the translucent slices with toast and condiments, as described here, or on cucumber slices with a dab of crème fraîche.

2 skin-on Arctic char fillets
(3/4 pound each)

1/2 cup kosher salt

1/4 cup raw (turbinado) sugar

1 1/2 tablespoons coriander seeds

2 teaspoons fennel seeds

Grated zest of 1 lemon

GARNISHES

Capers, thinly sliced or minced red onion, thinly sliced cucumber, fresh dill, crème fraîche, baguette toasts (page 41)

With needle-nose pliers or tweezers, remove the fish's fine pin bones. (You can feel these by running your fingers over the thickest part of the flesh in the head-to-tail direction.) In a small bowl, stir together the salt and sugar. Lightly crush the coriander and fennel seeds together in a mortar.

Line a tray with plastic wrap. Sprinkle the tray with 1/4 cup of the salt-sugar blend, making an evenly thick bed as large as the fillets will be when placed side by side. Arrange the fillets on the bed of seasoning, skin side down. Sprinkle each fillet with 1/4 cup of the salt-sugar blend and with half of the pounded seeds and half of the lemon zest. Sandwich the fillets, flesh sides together, then wrap tightly in plastic wrap. Put a tray on top and a 5-pound weight on the tray. Refrigerate for 24 hours, turning over the package halfway through.

Unwrap the fish and inspect the flesh. It should feel firm but not leathery. If it still feels flaccid, rewrap, replace the weight, and marinate for a few hours longer.

To serve, unwrap the fish and scrape off the spices. Rinse the flesh briefly in cold water, then pat it dry. Using a thin-bladed slicing knife, carve the fish as thinly as possible on a strong bias to make wide slices. Arrange the slices on a platter or on individual plates and pass the garnishes separately for guests to add as desired.

Enjoy with Cakebread Cellars Sauvignon Blanc or another medium-weight, brisk white wine.

Olive Oil–Fried Egg with Roasted Asparagus and Parmesan

SERVES 4

The affinity between asparagus and eggs is apparent to anyone who has ever enjoyed an asparagus omelet. But here's another variation on that theme. Brian roasts the asparagus to concentrate their flavor, then tops them with fried farm eggs basted with sizzling olive oil. The edges of the egg white become lacy and crisp while the yolk remains runny. A sprinkling of Parmesan helps make the dish more wine compatible. Serve as a first course for a spring dinner party, or in larger portions for a weeknight supper. It's best to fry only one egg at a time, but each one takes less than 30 seconds.

1½ pounds large asparagus

6 tablespoons extra-virgin olive oil

Kosher salt and freshly ground black pepper

1 cup thickly sliced spring onions or leeks, white and pale green parts only

4 large eggs, at room temperature

2 tablespoons freshly grated Parmesan cheese

Preheat the oven to 400°F. Snap off the woody ends of the asparagus. Arrange the spears on a baking sheet, drizzle with 2 tablespoons olive oil, and season with salt and pepper. Toss with your hands to coat the asparagus evenly with oil and seasonings, then rearrange in a single layer with tips pointing in the same direction. Roast in the middle of the oven until tender, about 15 minutes.

Heat 1 tablespoon olive oil in a small skillet over high heat. Add the onions and a pinch of salt. Cook, stirring to prevent browning, until wilted, about 2 minutes. Set aside.

About 1 minute before the asparagus is done, heat the remaining 3 tablespoons olive oil in a small nonstick skillet over high heat. When the oil is hot, crack an egg into a small bowl, then slide the egg into the hot oil. The egg white will immediately puff and sputter, so be careful. After about 30 seconds, remove the pan from the heat and spoon the hot oil over the egg to firm the white and film the yolk. Season with salt and pepper.

Divide the hot asparagus among 4 warm plates. Top one of the portions with the fried egg, lifting it out of the oil with a slotted spatula. Return the skillet to high heat and repeat with the remaining eggs; you should not need additional oil.

Garnish each portion with some of the sautéed onions and Parmesan, dividing them evenly. Serve immediately.

Enjoy with Cakebread Cellars Sauvignon Blanc or another young and brisk white wine.

New Potatoes with Goat Cheese and Tapenade

SERVES 8

Over the years, workshop chefs have devised many memorable hors d'oeuvres with chèvre because of Cakebread's long friendship with two wine-country goat cheese producers: Laura Chenel and Skyhill. This one-bite appetizer, featuring soft herbed goat cheese spread on a potato slice with a dollop of tapenade, comes from chef Pascal Olhats, who prepared it during the 1993 Workshop. If you have a small food processor, you can halve the tapenade recipe, as you need only a small amount for this dish. Then again, tapenade keeps well in the refrigerator, and you will be happy to have some on hand. Use it as a sandwich condiment or spread for crostini, slather it on grilled tuna, or toss it with pasta.

8 small red potatoes, about the size of golf balls (about 1/3 pound)

2 ounces fresh goat cheese

1 tablespoon fine dry bread crumbs

2 teaspoons extra-virgin olive oil

1/4 teaspoon minced fresh thyme

TAPENADE

1/2 pound pitted niçoise or kalamata olives (about 1 cup)

2 tablespoons extra-virgin olive oil

4 anchovy fillets

2 teaspoons capers, rinsed

1 large clove garlic, crushed

Pinch of freshly ground black pepper

Sprigs fresh thyme for garnish

Put the potatoes in a small saucepan with salted water to cover by 1 inch. Bring to a boil, adjust the heat to maintain a simmer, and cook until the potatoes are tender when pierced, about 15 minutes. Drain and let cool. Slice the potatoes about 1/4 inch thick, discarding the rounded ends. You should get 3 or 4 slices from each potato.

In a small bowl, combine the cheese, bread crumbs, olive oil, and thyme.

For the tapenade: Combine all the ingredients in a food processor and blend until smooth.

Preheat a broiler. Spread each potato slice with some of the cheese mixture, dividing it evenly, then put the slices on a tray and broil until the cheese melts and colors slightly, 2 to 3 minutes. Top each slice with about 1/4 teaspoon tapenade and garnish with the tip of a thyme sprig. Serve immediately.

Enjoy with Cakebread Cellars Sauvignon Blanc or another refreshing white wine or rosé.

Shrimp Corndogs with Bistro Honey Mustard

SERVES 8

Everyone's inner child emerges when these "corndogs" come out of the fryer. Who doesn't love eating from a skewer? But unlike the popular corndogs that star at America's state fairs, this whimsical hors d'oeuvre hides a juicy whole shrimp under its cornbread coat. Steven Oakley, a 2005 Workshop alumnus, serves the skewers with homemade honey mustard for dipping. On another occasion, you could use the cornmeal batter for pancakes.

1/3 cup Dijon mustard

1 tablespoon plus 1 teaspoon honey

CORNMEAL BATTER

2 cups all-purpose flour

1 cup plus 2 tablespoons yellow cornmeal

2 tablespoons sugar

1 tablespoon baking powder

1 teaspoon kosher salt

2 cups whole milk, or more as needed

1 large egg

1 large egg yolk

Vegetable oil for deep-frying

16 large shrimp (16–20 count), peeled and deveined

16 (6-inch) bamboo skewers

In a small bowl, stir together the mustard and honey. Set aside.

For the cornmeal batter: In a large bowl, whisk together the flour, cornmeal, sugar, baking powder, and salt. In another bowl, whisk together the milk, egg, and egg yolk. Add the liquid ingredients to the dry ingredients and whisk to blend. Thin the batter with a little more milk if batter is too stiff for coating the shrimp.

Heat 3 inches of vegetable oil in a deep pot to 375°F. Adjust the heat to maintain the temperature.

Using 1 skewer per shrimp, skewer each shrimp from tail to head end so that the shrimp is straight. Working in batches, dip the shrimp in batter to coat thoroughly, then place the whole skewer in the hot oil and fry until the cornmeal coating is golden brown, about 2 1/2 minutes. Transfer to paper towels to drain. Serve hot with a ramekin of honey mustard.

Enjoy with Cakebread Cellars Napa Valley Chardonnay or another full-bodied white wine.

From Sunlight to Sweetness

HELENE AND SPENCER MARSHALL maintain beehives all over the San Francisco Bay Area, including some in our vineyards. Thanks to the Marshalls, we have had several tutorials in beekeeping and honey harvesting and have come to appreciate that varietal honey can be as varied and distinctive as varietal wine. Pumpkin-blossom honey is assertive and dark, almost earthy in flavor, like Italian chestnut honey. Blackberry honey is sweeter and fruitier, while Napa wildflower honey is complex and delicious on wholewheat toast.

Often we take the Workshop participants to visit the hives in our vineyards. Spencer, the beekeeper, invites everyone to "suit up" while he smokes the hive to calm the bees so he can remove a frame. He explains how a hive operates, and often he locates and points out the queen. Breaking off fresh honeycomb and sampling it on the spot is a transporting taste experience, like eating a warm tomato right from the garden.

We always offer Marshall's Farm honey at the Workshop breakfasts. Participants drizzle it over Bellwether Farms ricotta or fromage blanc, and it tastes all the sweeter because they have met the bees who made it.

Rock Shrimp and Yuca Cakes with Spicy Mango Salad

SERVES 4

Crab cake fans will enjoy chef Marc Ehrler's golden shrimp cakes, a dish that reflects his years cooking in the Caribbean. Chef Ehrler, a 1991 Workshop participant, substitutes rock shrimp for crab, grated yuca for bread crumbs, and cilantro for parsley to make an appetizer that tastes like something you might find at a seafood shack on Martinique. A mango salad seasoned with chile and lime is the palate-tingling accompaniment. Look for yuca, the starchy root vegetable also known as cassava, in markets that cater to a Latin American or Caribbean clientele.

NOTE: Because the shrimp cakes must be served fresh and hot, it's helpful to prepare all the salad ingredients in advance so they can be quickly combined while the fried cakes are draining.

SALAD

½ large mango, peeled, cut into ½-inch dice

1 tablespoon finely minced red bell pepper

1 tablespoon finely minced red onion

1 tablespoon chopped fresh cilantro

¼ teaspoon seeded and finely minced habanero chile

2 tablespoons unseasoned rice vinegar

2 tablespoons extra-virgin olive oil

½ teaspoon grated lime zest

1 teaspoon freshly squeezed lime juice

¼ teaspoon kosher salt

SHRIMP CAKES

½ pound yuca (cassava)

6 ounces rock shrimp, finely minced

1 large egg, lightly beaten

2 tablespoons heavy cream

1 tablespoon chopped fresh cilantro

1 tablespoon finely minced red bell pepper

1 tablespoon finely minced red onion

¾ teaspoon kosher salt

Freshly ground black pepper

Vegetable oil for frying

2 ounces (2 large handfuls) baby greens

For the salad: In a large bowl, combine the mango, bell pepper, onion, cilantro, chile, rice vinegar, olive oil, lime zest, lime juice, and salt. Set aside.

For the shrimp cakes: Peel the yuca and cut it into 2-inch chunks. Put the chunks in a saucepan, cover with salted water, and bring to a boil over high heat. Simmer until you can just pierce the yuca with the tip of a paring knife, about 8 minutes. Drain and let cool. Grate on the coarse holes of a box grater. In a bowl, combine the grated yuca with the shrimp, egg, cream, cilantro, bell pepper, onion, salt, and a few grinds of pepper. Mix with your hands to blend. Divide the mixture into 8 equal portions. Shape each into a flattened cake about 3 inches in diameter.

Heat a 12-inch nonstick skillet over moderate heat. Add ¼ inch of the vegetable oil. When the oil is hot, add the shrimp cakes and fry until nicely browned on both sides, about 2½ minutes per side. Transfer to paper towels to drain briefly.

Add the greens to the salad mixture and toss. Taste and adjust the seasoning. Divide the salad among 4 salad plates. Put 2 shrimp cakes on each plate. Serve immediately.

Enjoy with Cakebread Cellars Sauvignon Blanc or another crisp and herbaceous white wine.

Grilled Peaches Wrapped in Serrano Ham

SERVES 8 TO 12

Like the marriage of prosciutto and melon, this duo explores the harmony of salty and sweet. Replace the peaches with nectarines, figs, or pears, if you prefer, or offer a combination. It's an easy, juicy hors d'oeuvre for a hot summer evening. Although you can wrap the charred fruit with prosciutto, the nutty, earthy serrano ham from Spain is less commonplace and may be a discovery for some of your guests. Don't wrap the fruit ahead or the ham will soften.

3 large freestone peaches (about 1 1/2 pounds)

1 tablespoon extra-virgin olive oil

1 teaspoon minced fresh thyme

1/2 teaspoon freshly cracked black pepper

3 ounces Spanish serrano ham or prosciutto, sliced paper thin

Prepare a hot charcoal fire or preheat a gas grill to high.

Cut each peach in half (no need to peel) and remove the pit. Slice each peach half into 3 or 4 wedges and toss with the olive oil, thyme, and pepper.

Grill the peaches on both cut sides until slightly softened, about 2 minutes per side, turning them with a spatula. Let the peaches cool to room temperature. Tear the ham lengthwise into as many pieces as you have peach wedges, then wrap a slice of ham around the center of each wedge, leaving the ends of each peach wedge exposed. Serve immediately.

Enjoy with Cakebread Cellars Vin de Porche Rosé or another dry or off-dry rosé.

Halibut *Crudo* with Shaved Radishes, Fried Capers, and Chive Oil

SERVES 8

Inspired by the simplicity and purity of Japanese sashimi, American chefs are exploring the world of seafood *crudo* (Italian for raw). Typically, *crudo* is accompanied by Mediterranean garnishes like capers and olive oil rather than the soy-based dipping sauce that is served with sashimi. At the 2005 Workshop, Florida chef James Reaux made a beautiful halibut *crudo* with chive oil, using the abundant chives in the winery garden. For raw preparations such as this one, the seafood must be impeccably fresh.

CHIVE OIL

1/4 cup thinly sliced fresh chives, plus more for garnish

1/2 cup extra-virgin olive oil

1 pound fresh center-cut skinless California halibut or fluke fillet

1 Meyer lemon, halved

1 teaspoon fleur de sel or sea salt

4 radishes, shaved with a vegetable slicer's julienne attachment or coarsely grated

Vegetable oil for frying

2 tablespoons large capers, rinsed and patted dry

For the chive oil: Put the chives and olive oil in a blender and puree until smooth. Transfer to a small bowl.

With a sharp knife, cut the halibut filet into broad, paper-thin slices, as if slicing smoked salmon. As you work, arrange the slices, slightly overlapping, on 8 chilled salad plates. You should be able to make about 32 slices, or 4 per portion. Drizzle the fish with Meyer lemon juice, using about 1 teaspoon per portion, then sprinkle with fleur de sel. Put a clump of shaved radish on the center of each portion, then drizzle chive oil around (not over) the fish, using about 2 teaspoons per portion.

In a small saucepan, heat about 1 inch of vegetable oil to 360°F. To test whether the oil is hot enough, add a couple of capers; they should sizzle on contact. Add all the capers and cook, stirring with a wire-mesh skimmer, until they stop sizzling fiercely, about 20 seconds. Transfer to paper towels with the skimmer. The buds should have opened slightly, and they should be crisp. Scatter over the fish and serve immediately.

Enjoy with Cakebread Cellars Sauvignon Blanc or another brisk, refreshing white wine.

Kabocha Squash *Panna Cotta*

SERVES 6

This modern, savory interpretation of *panna cotta* comes from Chef Debbie Gold, who participated in the 2000 Workshop. It has the silky, quivery texture of a traditional dessert *panna cotta*, with an appetizing butterscotch color. For an autumn first course, serve the custard with crisp toasts and a tart salad for contrast. Note that the *panna cotta* must be chilled for at least four hours before serving.

PANNA COTTA

1½ teaspoons unflavored gelatin

1 cup whole milk, divided

¾ cup heavy cream

½ cup roasted kabocha squash puree (see Notes)

2 teaspoons chopped fresh thyme

¾ teaspoon kosher salt

Freshly ground white pepper

BAGUETTE TOASTS

18 thin baguette slices, cut on a strong diagonal

Extra-virgin olive oil

SALAD

1 to 2 heads baby frisée (about ¼ pound total)

2 tablespoons extra-virgin olive oil

2 tablespoons golden balsamic vinegar or cider vinegar

¼ cup coarsely chopped marcona almonds (see Notes)

Kosher salt

For the *panna cotta*: In a small bowl, sprinkle the gelatin over ¼ cup of the milk. Let soften for 5 minutes. Place the remaining ¾ cup milk, the cream, squash, and thyme in a saucepan. Whisk to blend. Warm over moderate heat just until it begins to simmer. Do not allow the mixture to boil.

Remove from the heat and add the softened gelatin, stirring until the gelatin dissolves. Season with salt and pepper. Strain through a fine-mesh sieve into a bowl. Let cool to room temperature, stirring occasionally. (You can speed up the cooling by placing the bowl in an ice bath.) Divide among 6 espresso cups or other small ramekins. Cover with plastic wrap and refrigerate for at least 4 hours or overnight.

For the baguette toasts: Preheat the oven to 400°F. Brush the baguette slices lightly with olive oil on both sides. Bake until golden and crisp, 10 to 12 minutes.

For the salad: Trim the core and any dark green outer leaves and leaf tips from the frisée. Tear the pale yellow center leaves into bite-size pieces. Just before serving, put the frisée in a bowl and toss with the olive oil, vinegar, almonds, and a pinch of salt.

To serve, put a *panna cotta* ramekin on each of 6 salad plates. Accompany each portion with 3 toasts and a tuft of frisée salad.

NOTES: For the kabocha squash puree, preheat the oven to 400°F. Cut a small kabocha squash in half and remove the seeds. Put one half in a pie tin or small baking dish, cut side down, reserving the other half for another use. Add ½ inch of water. Bake until the squash feels tender when probed, about 45 minutes. Let cool, then scoop the flesh from the skin into a bowl. Stir with a wooden spoon until smooth, then measure out ½ cup.

Marcona almonds are Spanish almonds that are typically skinned, fried in oil, and salted. They are available at well-stocked grocery stores and specialty food stores. For a substitute, toast whole blanched almonds, then toss with olive oil and salt.

Enjoy with Cakebread Cellars Chardonnay Reserve or another rich, barrel-fermented Chardonnay.

Cucumber Cups with Roasted Beets and Yogurt Dressing

SERVES 8

The beets and cucumbers in Dolores's summer garden and the tangy goat's-milk yogurt from Skyhill Farms, a Napa Valley producer, inspired chef William Withrow at the 2005 Workshop. He folded diced roasted beets into yogurt, then spooned the mixture into edible "cups" made from cucumber chunks. When all of the ingredients are well chilled, this healthful appetizer is incomparably refreshing—just what you want on a warm summer night.

1 medium red or golden beet

3 tablespoons whole-milk yogurt

1 teaspoon minced fresh dill, plus dill sprigs for garnish

1 teaspoon very finely minced shallots

Kosher salt and freshly ground white pepper

1 Armenian or English (hothouse) cucumber

Preheat the oven to 400°F. Wrap the beet loosely in aluminum foil, sealing the package tightly. Bake until the beet is tender when pierced, about 1 hour. When cool enough to handle, peel the beet and cut it into very small, neat dice. You should have about $1/2$ cup.

Place the diced beet in a small bowl and fold in the yogurt, minced dill, and shallots. Season to taste with salt and white pepper. Chill well.

Peel the cucumber and cut into $1/2$-inch-wide chunks. You should have about 2 dozen. Use a melon baller to scoop out the center of each chunk to make room for a filling, taking care not to pierce the bottom and to leave the sides about $1/4$ inch thick. Set the cucumber cups on a serving tray and chill. Just before filling, season with salt and white pepper.

To serve, spoon 1 teaspoon of the beet mixture into each cucumber cup and garnish with a small sprig of dill. Serve immediately.

Enjoy with Cakebread Cellars Sauvignon Blanc or another young, dry white wine with good acidity.

Fried Green Tomatoes with Goat Cheese and Fennel Marmalade

SERVES 8

By mid-November, the tomato vines in our garden have usually had enough. The days are no longer sufficiently warm to ripen the fruits that remain on the plants, so we start thinking about fried green tomatoes. Southerners might raise their eyebrows, but Brian uses neither cornmeal nor bacon fat when he makes these. He prefers the lightness of vegetable oil and the crispness of a panko coating. These coarse Japanese bread crumbs are a favorite of many chefs because they produce such a crunchy and well-browned exterior. Brian tops the fried tomatoes with a dollop of softened goat cheese from Skyhill Farms and a spoonful of fennel marmalade. The dish offers so many pleasing contrasts: warm and cool, tart and sweet, crisp and creamy. We typically serve it as a passed hors d'oeuvre with our Sauvignon Blanc, which has the bright acidity to match.

FENNEL MARMALADE

2 tablespoons extra-virgin olive oil

1 fennel bulb, minced

1 yellow onion, minced

4 sprigs fresh thyme

2 strips of lemon zest

2 teaspoons Pernod

Freshly squeezed lemon juice

Kosher salt

4 green (underripe) tomatoes, sliced 1/2 inch thick

1 cup unbleached all-purpose flour

3 large eggs, beaten

1/2 cup buttermilk

2 cups panko (packaged Japanese bread crumbs)

Vegetable oil for frying

4 ounces fresh goat cheese, at room temperature

1 tablespoon minced fresh chives

For the fennel marmalade: In a small saucepan, place the olive oil, fennel, onion, thyme sprigs, and lemon zest. Cover and cook over moderate heat, stirring occasionally, until the fennel and onion are meltingly tender, about 20 minutes. Do not let them brown. Uncover and continue cooking until most of the moisture has evaporated, about 5 minutes. Add the Pernod and cook uncovered, stirring, for about 2 minutes to evaporate the alcohol. Remove from the heat and discard the thyme sprigs. Pull out the strips of lemon zest, mince fine, and return to the mixture. Season to taste with lemon juice and salt. Let cool to room temperature.

Season the tomato slices on both sides with salt.

Set up a breading station: Put the flour in a small bowl. Combine the eggs and buttermilk in another bowl and whisk to blend. Put the panko in a third bowl. Using one hand for the wet mixture and another for the dry ingredients (the flour and the panko), dip the tomato slices first in flour, coating both sides. Drop the floured tomato into the egg mixture and, using your "wet" hand, turn it to coat it with egg. With your "wet" hand, place the coated tomato on the bread crumbs. Use your "dry" hand to press the bread crumbs into place on both sides. Place the coated tomatoes on a tray in a single layer.

Put 1/4 inch of vegetable oil in a 12- to 14-inch skillet and set over high heat. When the oil begins to shimmer, dip the edge of a coated tomato slice in the oil. If it sizzles on contact, the oil is hot enough; if not, wait a little longer.

Add the tomatoes to the skillet a few at a time; do not crowd them. Fry on both sides, turning with tongs, until golden brown, about 1 minute per side. Lower the heat if needed to keep the bread crumbs from burning. Transfer the fried tomatoes as they are done to a double thickness of paper towels to drain. Season with another pinch of salt.

Put the goat cheese in a bowl and mash with the back of a spoon until smooth. Arrange the fried tomatoes on a serving tray. Top each tomato with a small spoonful of goat cheese, then top the goat cheese with 1 teaspoon of fennel marmalade. Sprinkle with chives and serve immediately.

Enjoy with Cakebread Cellars Sauvignon Blanc or another dry, refreshing white wine.

Chèvre as Fresh as It Gets

WHEN YOU'RE BUYING RINDLESS, unripened chèvre, freshness matters. This moist cheese is meant to be consumed immediately, so we don't want to purchase it from across the country, much less from across the sea.

Fortunately, we have a producer practically in our own backyard, Skyhill Napa Valley Farms. Proprietor Amy Wend started with three goats in 1990 and now has a herd of almost 450. Her creamy chèvre is a staple at the winery, and because we receive it almost as soon as she makes it, the chèvre tastes as lively, clean, and fresh as the goat's milk it came from.

We use Skyhill chèvre on crostini topped with beet tartare, on pizza, crumbled into salads, or in galettes with tomato or summer squash. Skyhill also makes an all-natural goat yogurt that often inspires the Workshop chefs. One year, Florida chef Oliver Saucy used it in a yogurt sorbet to accompany his Peach Crisp with Crystallized Ginger and Pecans (page 178). Another time, California chef William Withrow used the yogurt to dress finely diced beets that he spooned into cucumber "cups" (page 42), an hors d'oeuvre we still make at the winery.

Smoked Trout Mousse with Apple-Fennel Salad

SERVES 8

At the winery, we are always looking for enticing finger foods that our guests can enjoy comfortably with a glass of wine in hand. This hors d'oeuvre from Memphis chef Wally Joe, devised at the 2004 Workshop, passes that test. Piped or spooned onto endive leaves, the mousse makes an easily passed hors d'oeuvre. The mousse's creamy texture and smoky notes find an echo in our Napa Valley Chardonnay, and the apple garnish provides another aromatic link.

SMOKED TROUT MOUSSE

1 skinless smoked trout fillet, about 1/4 pound

1/4 cup crème fraîche

1/4 cup heavy cream

1 teaspoon freshly squeezed lemon juice

1/4 teaspoon prepared horseradish

1 tablespoon thinly sliced fresh chives

Freshly ground black pepper

APPLE-FENNEL SALAD

1/2 small tart apple, such as Granny Smith, peeled and cut into 1/4-inch dice

1/4 small fennel bulb, cored, cut into 1/4-inch dice

1 1/2 teaspoons chopped fennel fronds, plus more whole fronds for garnish

1 tablespoon extra-virgin olive oil

1 teaspoon cider vinegar

1 teaspoon honey

Kosher salt

2 dozen Belgian endive leaves

For the mousse: By hand, break the trout into flakes, removing any bones. In a food processor, puree the trout, crème fraîche, cream, lemon juice, and horseradish until smooth, about 2 minutes. Transfer to a bowl, stir in the chives and several grinds of pepper, then refrigerate until the mixture is firm enough to pipe through a pastry bag, about 30 minutes.

For the salad: In a small bowl, combine the apple, fennel, chopped fennel fronds, olive oil, vinegar, honey, and a pinch of salt. Toss well.

If necessary, trim the base of the endive leaves so each leaf is no longer than 3 inches.

Using a pastry bag fitted with a 1/2-inch plain tip, pipe about 2 teaspoons of mousse onto each endive leaf. Alternatively, use a spoon to place about 2 teaspoons of the mousse on each leaf. Top with a small spoonful of the apple-fennel salad. Garnish each filled leaf with a small fennel frond.

Enjoy with Cakebread Cellars Napa Valley Chardonnay or another creamy, barrel-aged Chardonnay.

Warm Chopped Liver Crostini with White Truffle Oil

MAKES 16 CROSTINI

Chef Nancy Oakes used fresh duck livers from Sonoma County Poultry when she made these elegant crostini during the 1997 Workshop, but chicken livers work, too. She hand-chopped the warm sautéed livers with butter and a lot of sweet sautéed onion, plus just enough earthy truffle oil to make them worthy of a black-tie occasion.

1/2 pound fresh chicken or duck livers

Kosher salt

2 tablespoons olive oil

1/2 large yellow onion, finely diced

1/2 teaspoon minced fresh sage

Freshly ground black pepper

2 tablespoons unsalted butter, at room temperature

About 1/2 teaspoon white truffle oil

FRIED SAGE GARNISH (OPTIONAL)

Vegetable oil for frying

16 large fresh sage leaves

16 baguette toasts (page 41)

Separate the lobes of the livers and discard any fat or veins. In a colander set over a bowl, toss the livers with 2 tablespoons salt. Let stand for 20 minutes to drain blood. Rinse the livers thoroughly in cold water, then pat dry.

Heat 1 tablespoon olive oil in a small nonstick skillet over moderately low heat. Add the onion and a pinch of salt and sauté until soft and translucent, about 20 minutes; do not let the onion brown. Transfer the onion to a bowl. Add the remaining 1 tablespoon olive oil to the same skillet and raise the heat to medium. When the oil is hot, add the livers, sage, and several grinds of black pepper. Sauté just until the livers feel firm but not hard, about 4 minutes. They should still be pink inside. Add the livers to the onions and let cool until just warm. Chop the liver and onions together until fine, adding the butter as you chop. Season the mixture to taste with salt, pepper, and truffle oil.

For the garnish: Heat 1/2 inch of vegetable oil in a small saucepan over medium heat. When the oil is hot enough to sizzle when you insert the end of a wooden chopstick, add the sage leaves, a few at a time. Be careful: they will pop and splatter. Cook until the leaves become crisp, about 30 seconds. Do not let them color. Transfer them with a slotted spoon to paper towels to drain briefly.

Spread the chopped liver on baguette toasts and top with a fried sage leaf. Serve immediately.

Enjoy with Cakebread Cellars Chardonnay Reserve or another full-bodied, barrel-fermented white wine.

Thai Stone Crab Tostadas

SERVES 8

To show off Florida's most famous shellfish, Chef Marty Blitz made miniature Thai-style tostadas at the Workshop in 1994. He replaced the conventional fried tortillas with wonton wrappers, which puff and crisp in the fryer and turn a rich nut-brown. Then he topped this crunchy base with a tangy crab and cabbage slaw sparked with fish sauce, lime juice, and chile. It's finger food, but drippy. Offer sturdy napkins or small plates. If you dislike deep-frying, spoon the slaw into Bibb lettuce cups or Belgian endive leaves. You could also omit the wonton wrappers and serve the slaw in generous portions for lunch, or offer it as a side dish with baked or fried fish.

FRIED WONTONS

Vegetable oil for frying

8 wonton wrappers, halved on the diagonal to make 16 triangles

1 cup stone crab meat (from about 1 pound cooked crab claws) or Dungeness crab meat

1½ cups very finely sliced green cabbage

2 tablespoons minced red onion

2 tablespoons thinly sliced scallions

DRESSING

2 tablespoons Thai fish sauce

1 tablespoon unseasoned rice vinegar

1 tablespoon freshly squeezed lime juice

1 teaspoon sugar

1 teaspoon finely grated fresh ginger

½ jalapeño chile, seeded and minced

Coarsely chopped fresh cilantro for garnish

For the fried wontons: In a 4-quart saucepan, heat 3 inches of vegetable oil to 375°F. Fry the wonton wrappers a few at a time, turning them once with tongs, until they puff and turn golden, less than a minute. Drain on a rack or paper towels.

In a bowl, combine the crab meat with the cabbage, red onion, and scallions.

For the dressing: In a small bowl, whisk together the fish sauce, rice vinegar, lime juice, sugar, ginger, and chile.

Add the dressing to the slaw and toss well. Put a spoonful of slaw on each wonton wrapper. Garnish with chopped cilantro and serve immediately.

Enjoy with Cakebread Cellars Sauvignon Blanc or another crisp white wine. An off-dry white wine would also work with these sweet-tart Asian flavors.

Caramelized Onion and Walnut Biscuits with Blue Cheese Butter

MAKES 20 TO 24 BISCUITS

For large parties, it's useful to have a repertoire of easy hors d'oeuvres that guests can enjoy standing up, with no plate or silverware. Winery chef Tom Sixsmith developed these tender biscuits for the wine and food program at our Visitors Center, where guests can sample appetizers designed to complement our wines. The toasted walnuts in these savory biscuits and the blue cheese butter inside help soften the tannins in our robust hillside Cabernet Sauvignon.

To save time, we make the biscuit dough in large batches, cut out the biscuits, and freeze them unbaked. Then we bring them to room temperature and bake them as needed so our guests have warm, buttery biscuits with their red wine. You could also serve them as an accompaniment to a green salad or a vegetable soup.

CARAMELIZED ONIONS

2 tablespoons extra-virgin olive oil

1 tablespoon unsalted butter, at room temperature

1 large yellow onion, minced

1/4 teaspoon kosher salt

2 teaspoons minced fresh thyme

2 1/2 cups all-purpose flour

2 teaspoons baking powder

1 teaspoon kosher salt

6 tablespoons unsalted butter, cut into 1/2-inch cubes and chilled

1/2 cup chopped toasted walnuts

1 large egg, beaten

2/3 cup whole milk

BLUE CHEESE BUTTER

4 to 5 ounces Point Reyes Original Blue or other blue cheese, at room temperature

3 tablespoons unsalted butter, at room temperature

For the caramelized onions: Heat the olive oil and butter in a small saucepan over medium heat. Add the onion and salt and cook, stirring occasionally, until the onion begins to caramelize and brown, 15 to 20 minutes. Lower the heat as needed to prevent burning. Stir in the thyme and remove from the heat. Let cool.

Preheat the oven to 425°F. In a bowl, whisk together the flour, baking powder, and salt. Add the chilled butter and mix in with a pastry blender or your fingertips until the butter is the size of small peas. Add the caramelized onions and the walnuts and mix gently with your hands.

In a small bowl, whisk together the egg and the milk. Make a well in the center of the dry ingredients, pour the egg mixture into the well, then mix gently with a rubber pastry scraper or spatula. The mixture will be shaggy; it will not come together into a smooth dough.

Line a baking sheet with parchment paper or a silicone mat. Turn the mixture out onto a lightly floured surface and knead gently until it forms a cohesive dough. Do not overwork or the biscuits will be tough. Pat or roll the dough into a round about 1 inch thick, flouring lightly as needed to prevent sticking. Cut out the biscuits with a lightly floured 1 1/2-inch round cutter. Place the biscuits on the prepared baking sheet. You can gather and reroll the scraps once. Refrigerate the biscuits for 15 minutes, then bake until golden brown, about 18 minutes. Let cool for 10 minutes.

For the blue cheese butter: In a small bowl, mash the blue cheese and the butter with the back of a spoon until the mixture is spreadable.

Cut the warm biscuits in half horizontally and spread the bottom half with a little of the blue cheese butter. Replace the top half. Arrange on a platter and serve warm.

Enjoy with Cakebread Cellars Dancing Bear Ranch Cabernet Sauvignon or another powerful red wine from Bordeaux varieties.

Blue Cheese, Red Wine

MOST MEALS AT CAKEBREAD CELLARS end, not with dessert, but with a cheese board, and Point Reyes Original Blue is often on it. We like the way a cheese board encourages sharing and lingering at the table, and of course we really like that it calls for another glass of wine.

In the interest of adding variety to our cheese boards, we have sampled numerous blue cheeses over the years. Many are too pungent, salty, or piquant to pair with red wine, but Original Blue works. Made in coastal Marin County by the Giacomini family, it has the creaminess and relatively mellow nature to complement our Cabernet Sauvignon.

Bob and Dean Giacomini have operated a dairy farm in scenic Point Reyes Station since 1959. But when it came time to pass the business to the next generation, the Giacominis' four daughters had other ideas. They didn't want to run a dairy farm, but converting the milk into artisan cheese had some appeal. So they hired an expert cheesemaker and, in 2000, debuted Point Reyes Original Blue, a rindless raw-milk wheel matured for six months.

Brian sometimes uses it in an endive and blue cheese galette, or in a fall salad with endive, persimmons, and caramelized walnuts. At the 2009 Workshop, chef Rob Wilson showcased Original Blue in a delicate soufflé.

SOUPS AND SALADS

SPRING

SUMMER

FALL

WINTER

Manila Clams, Arugula, and White Beans with Preserved Lemon Vinaigrette

SERVES 6

Although you might think of cooked beans as red-wine food, when they're tossed with shellfish, greens, and a lemony dressing, they pair better with Sauvignon Blanc. Brian created this recipe for a Workshop session on wine and food matching, to demonstrate how ingredients like citrus and arugula can steer a dish toward white wine. Note that you need to soak the beans overnight.

BEANS

1/2 pound large dried white beans, such as Rancho Gordo cannellini beans (opposite page)

1 small carrot, peeled, cut into large chunks

1/2 small yellow onion, cut into 3 pieces

1 celery rib

1 bay leaf

Kosher salt

2 pounds manila clams

2 tablespoons extra-virgin olive oil

2 cloves garlic, minced

Pinch of red chile flakes

1/2 cup Cakebread Cellars Sauvignon Blanc

VINAIGRETTE

1/4 cup freshly squeezed lemon juice

1 tablespoon minced rind of preserved lemons (page 192)

1 tablespoon chopped fresh oregano

1/2 cup extra-virgin olive oil

3 ounces (3 large handfuls) baby arugula

For the beans: Soak the beans overnight in water to cover generously. Drain and transfer them to a large saucepan. Add fresh water to cover by 2 inches. Add the carrot, onion, celery, and bay leaf. Bring to a boil over high heat, skimming any foam. Reduce the heat to maintain a gentle simmer and cook, uncovered, until the beans are tender, about 1 hour, depending on age. Season to taste with salt and let the beans cool in the liquid. Discard the carrot, onion, celery, and bay leaf.

Cover the clams generously with cold water and let stand for 20 minutes to release sand. Lift them out of the water, leaving behind any grit.

Heat the olive oil in a large pot over high heat. Add the garlic and chile flakes and sauté briefly to release the garlic fragrance. Add the wine and the clams. Cover and cook until the clams open, about 3 minutes. Transfer the clams to a bowl, discarding any that fail to open. Strain the liquid through a double thickness of cheesecloth to remove any grit.

For the vinaigrette: In a bowl, combine the lemon juice, preserved lemon rind, and oregano. Add 2 tablespoons of the strained clam broth. Whisk in the olive oil. Season with salt.

Drain the beans and put them in a large bowl. Add enough vinaigrette to coat them and let them sit for 20 minutes to absorb the seasonings. Add the arugula and clams and toss again, adding more vinaigrette as needed. Taste and adjust the seasoning. Serve immediately.

Enjoy with Cakebread Cellars Sauvignon Blanc or another crisp, dry white wine without obvious oak.

Beans Worth a Star Turn

CONSUMERS SWOON OVER THE SHAPES and colors of heirloom tomatoes, but few people have the same response to dried beans. Many cooks think of beans as a generic commodity, like flour or sugar, and blame themselves when the dried beans they buy at the supermarket don't cook evenly or taste like much.

Thanks to Steve Sando of Rancho Gordo, we now have dried beans worth swooning over. Brian met Steve at the Napa farmers' market, where his display of speckled, mottled, and whimsically named beans could not help turning heads. Steve grew them himself at first, but he now has a network of farmers who produce the beans for him, including some growers in Mexico. These old-fashioned beauties have names like Good Mother Stallard and Yellow Indian Woman, and they have survived because backyard gardeners or small-scale farmers prized them, saved them, and passed them down. The first time Brian made a pot of some mottled pinto beans that he got from Rancho Gordo, Brenda Godinez, a winery staffer, recognized them as the *flor de junio* ("June flower") beans esteemed in her hometown in the Mexican state of Michoacán.

Brian prefers to cook Rancho Gordo beans in water, not stock, to let their distinctive personalities emerge. The full-flavored broth they produce is a treasure in its own right. The beans cook uniformly and more quickly than you might expect because they are always from the most recent crop and haven't been stored in a warehouse for too long.

We love introducing Workshop chefs to these beans and seeing the creativity they inspire. Several participants have done riffs on cassoulet; Rick Moonen made a bean chili paired with salmon. Brian sometimes makes a Rancho Gordo bean puree to use as a base for sautéed pork or lamb; the creamy beans make a sauce unnecessary. For the winery employees' pre-harvest party, he makes a big pot of Rancho Gordo beans flavored with chorizo from the Fatted Calf, a respected local charcuterie producer.

Carrot, Fennel, and Green Olive Slaw

SERVES 4 TO 6

Brian likes to serve this slaw with Moroccan Lamb Brochettes (page 124), but it would also complement grilled swordfish, fish brochettes, or grilled sausages. Sometimes, at home with his family, he buys spicy *merguez* (lamb sausages) from a local merchant, grills them, and tucks them into a baguette with aioli and this crunchy slaw. Choose firm green olives, such as picholines. The texture will be better if you buy the olives unpitted and pit them yourself.

1 pound carrots, ends trimmed

1 fennel bulb, halved, cored, and very thinly sliced

1 cup pitted and halved green olives, such as picholines, rinsed if salty

1/3 cup extra-virgin olive oil

2 tablespoons freshly squeezed lemon juice

1/4 cup coarsely chopped cilantro

1 tablespoon coarsely chopped fresh mint

Kosher salt and freshly ground pepper

With a mandoline or other manual vegetable slicer fitted with a medium (not fine) julienne attachment, julienne the carrots. Alternatively, by hand, cut the carrots thinly on the diagonal into elongated coins, then stack the coins and cut into 1/4-inch-wide strips.

In a large bowl, toss together the carrots, fennel, and olives. Add the olive oil, lemon juice, cilantro, and mint. Season to taste with salt and pepper. Let stand for about 45 minutes to allow the carrots to soften slightly.

Butter Lettuce Salad with Avocado Ranch Dressing

SERVES 6

Chef Alan Greeley, who attended the 1997 Workshop, introduced us to this luscious salad dressing. Inspired by the creamy "ranch dressing" that originated on a dude ranch in Santa Barbara, Alan's version incorporates avocado for an even silkier texture. He pairs the dressing with steamed artichokes and asparagus; we love it on tender leaves of butter lettuce with a shower of fresh spring herbs from our garden.

AVOCADO RANCH DRESSING

1 large avocado, peeled and pitted

1/2 cup mayonnaise

1/2 cup buttermilk

1/4 cup thinly sliced scallions (green parts only)

3 tablespoons freshly squeezed lemon juice, or more to taste

1 teaspoon chopped fresh tarragon

Kosher salt and cayenne pepper, to taste

2 large or 3 small heads butter lettuce

1 tablespoon thinly sliced fresh chives

1 tablespoon chopped flat-leaf parsley

2 large hard-boiled eggs, coarsely chopped

Half-pint cherry tomatoes, halved

For the dressing: In a food processor, combine all the ingredients and puree until smooth and creamy.

Core the lettuce heads and separate them into individual leaves. In a large bowl, toss the lettuce leaves with enough of the dressing to coat them lightly; you may not need it all. Arrange the lettuce on a platter. Sprinkle with chives and parsley, then with chopped egg. Scatter the cherry tomatoes around the lettuce. Serve immediately.

Enjoy with Cakebread Cellars Napa Valley Chardonnay or another elegant, cool-climate Chardonnay.

Watermelon and Tomato Gazpacho

SERVES 8

At the 2001 Workshop, Chef Ken Vedrinski astonished guests with a "consommé" made from the strained juice of tomatoes and watermelon. Preparing the dish involved hanging the pureed fruits in a muslin bag overnight to collect the clear, sweet juices—a procedure that might deter many home cooks. Riffing on Chef Vedrinski's idea, Brian created an easier gazpacho that blends tomato, watermelon, and other summer vegetables so seamlessly that you can't decipher the contents. The result is a refreshing and original adaptation of the familiar Spanish soup.

1½ cups crustless day-old bread, in ½-inch cubes

1½ pounds ripe tomatoes, peeled, halved, seeded, and coarsely chopped

2 to 2½ cups peeled watermelon, in 1-inch cubes

½ English (hothouse) cucumber, peeled, halved lengthwise, seeded, and coarsely chopped

½ large red bell pepper, halved and seeded

½ fennel bulb, halved, cored, and coarsely chopped

¼ small red onion, coarsely chopped

3 tablespoons extra-virgin olive oil, plus more for garnish

2 tablespoons sherry vinegar, or to taste

Kosher salt

¼ cup finely diced watermelon for garnish

Put the bread in a bowl, cover with cold water, and let soak for 15 minutes. Drain and squeeze dry.

In a blender in batches, puree the bread, tomatoes, watermelon, cucumber, bell pepper, fennel, onion, olive oil, vinegar, and enough water to achieve a pleasing consistency (about 1 cup). Season with salt and add more vinegar if necessary. Chill thoroughly.

Divide the soup among 8 bowls. Garnish each serving with a spoonful of diced watermelon. Drizzle with extra-virgin olive oil. Serve immediately.

Enjoy with Cakebread Cellars Vin de Porche Rosé or another dry rosé.

Provençal Garlic and Saffron Soup

SERVES 4

Hubert Keller, chef-owner of San Francisco's Fleur de Lys, patterned this recipe after the traditional Provençal *soupe doux* (sweet garlic soup), a specialty of the peasant kitchen. But as you might expect from a chef for one of the city's most elegant restaurants, Chef Keller has refined the procedure, blanching the garlic to temper some of its bite and adding saffron for a richer color. A poached egg set on a crouton in the center of the soup really dresses up the dish. Chef Keller participated in the 1991 Workshop.

3 whole heads garlic, cloves separated and peeled

2 tablespoons extra-virgin olive oil

2 cups sliced leeks, white and pale green part only

1 Yukon Gold potato (about 4 ounces), peeled, cut into 1/2-inch chunks

1 quart vegetable stock (page 191)

1/2 teaspoon saffron threads

Kosher salt and freshly ground white pepper

1/4 cup heavy cream or half-and-half

GARLIC TOASTS

4 baguette slices, about 3/4 inch thick

Extra-virgin olive oil

1 clove garlic, halved

POACHED EGGS

1 tablespoon white wine vinegar

4 large eggs

2 tablespoons finely sliced fresh chives for garnish

Piment d'Espelette (Basque ground red pepper) or paprika for garnish

Put the peeled garlic cloves in a small saucepan with cold water to cover. Bring to a boil, drain, then repeat the blanching two times.

Heat the olive oil in a large pot over moderate heat. Add the leeks and sauté, stirring often, until wilted, about 5 minutes. Add the blanched garlic, potato, stock, saffron, and salt and pepper to taste. Bring to a simmer and cook until the potato is soft, about 15 minutes. Remove from the heat and let cool slightly.

Transfer the soup to a blender or food processor, in batches if necessary, and puree until smooth. Return the soup to a clean saucepan. Stir in the cream. Taste and adjust the seasoning.

For the garlic toasts: Preheat the oven to 400°F. Brush the baguette slices lightly with olive oil on both sides. Bake until golden, 10 to 12 minutes. Rub lightly with the halved garlic.

For the poached eggs: Bring 3 inches of salted water to a boil in a large pot over high heat. Add the vinegar and reduce the heat to maintain the water just below a simmer. Crack 1 egg into a small ramekin or bowl, then gently slip it into the water. With a slotted spoon, gather the white around the yolk. Repeat with the remaining eggs. Cook gently until the whites are firm but the yolks remain soft, about 3 minutes. Transfer the eggs with a slotted spoon to paper towels or a clean dish towel to drain briefly.

To serve, reheat the soup if necessary. Put a toast in the bottom of each soup bowl. Top with a poached egg, then ladle the soup around it. Garnish with a sprinkle of chives and a dash of *piment d'Espelette*. Serve immediately.

Enjoy with Cakebread Cellars Napa Valley Chardonnay or another white wine with lush texture.

Lobster and Melon Salad with Hazelnut Oil

SERVES 6

Canadian chef Jonathan Gushue, a 2008 Workshop participant, introduced us to the notion of pairing lobster with melon—a clever juxtaposition of rich with lean. The cool juiciness of the melon balances the lobster's buttery sweetness, so the salad seems refreshing and light. Serve it as the first course of a seafood dinner or, in larger portions, as a summer lunch.

VINAIGRETTE

1 small shallot, finely minced

1 tablespoon sherry vinegar

1/2 teaspoon Dijon mustard

1/4 teaspoon honey

2 tablespoons extra-virgin olive oil

1 tablespoon hazelnut oil

Kosher salt and freshly ground black pepper

2 live lobsters (11/4 to 11/2 pounds each)

1/4 cantaloupe or other orange-fleshed melon, seeds and rind removed

1/4 honeydew or other green-fleshed melon, seeds and rind removed

2 ounces (about 2 large handfuls) baby arugula

1/4 cup coarsely chopped toasted hazelnuts for garnish

4 large fresh mint leaves, chopped, for garnish

For the vinaigrette: In a small bowl, combine the shallot, vinegar, mustard, and honey. Whisk in the oils gradually. Season with salt and pepper.

For the lobsters: Put 2 gallons cold water in a stockpot with 1/2 cup salt. Bring to a boil over high heat. Add the lobsters and cover. When the water returns to a boil, uncover and boil for 12 minutes. Transfer the lobsters to ice water to chill quickly.

Twist off the lobster tail, knuckles, and claws; discard the rest of the carcass. Crack open the shell of the tail and remove the meat in one piece, or use your finger or a small fork to push the meat out through the larger end. Crack the knuckle shells and remove the meat. To extract the meat from the claw, jiggle the small lower appendage until it snaps, then remove it. Crack the shell of the claw and pull out the meat in one piece, if possible. Cut the tail into 1/2-inch chunks and cut the knuckle meat into 2 or 3 pieces. Leave the claws whole.

Slice the melon quarters thinly lengthwise, then cut each slice crosswise into thirds.

Put the lobster in a bowl with the melon. Toss with the vinaigrette, using as much as you need to moisten the lobster and fruit. Add the arugula and more dressing, if needed, and toss again. Divide among individual plates or arrange on a platter. Garnish with hazelnuts and mint. Serve immediately.

Enjoy with Cakebread Cellars Napa Valley Chardonnay or another full-bodied white wine.

Heirloom Tomato Salad with Roasted-Garlic Vinaigrette and Chèvre-Stuffed Piquillo Peppers

SERVES 6

The Workshop coincides with sweet pepper season, and many chefs are seduced by the varieties they find in our garden. Chef Donald Barickman, a 2000 Workshop participant, succumbed to the small, sweet 'Lipstick' peppers—so named for their crimson color—which he roasted and stuffed with creamy goat cheese and served with arugula and roasted-garlic vinaigrette. Bottled Spanish piquillo peppers make a good substitute. Brian adds heirloom tomatoes to make a more substantial composed salad for the end of summer. Serve it before or alongside grilled lamb, sausage, or burgers.

ROASTED-GARLIC VINAIGRETTE

6 large cloves garlic, peeled

1/3 cup plus 1 teaspoon extra-virgin olive oil

Kosher salt and freshly ground black pepper

2 tablespoons cider vinegar

1 small shallot, minced

1 teaspoon Dijon mustard

6 bottled Spanish piquillo peppers (see page 193)

4 ounces soft fresh goat cheese, at room temperature

2 tablespoons finely chopped toasted pecans

1 tablespoon sliced fresh chives

1 teaspoon chopped flat-leaf parsley

1 small clove garlic, mashed to a paste with a pinch of salt

2 pounds heirloom tomatoes

1/2 cup fresh basil leaves

4 ounces (about 4 handfuls) mixed lettuces

1/2 cup coarsely chopped toasted pecans

For the vinaigrette: Preheat the oven to 400°F. Put the garlic cloves on a square of aluminum foil. Add the 1 teaspoon olive oil and season with salt and pepper; toss to coat. Seal the foil around the garlic to make a package and bake until the garlic is tender, about 40 minutes. On a cutting board, mash the garlic to a paste with the side of a chef's knife. In a small bowl, whisk together the vinegar, shallot, mustard, and garlic paste. Whisk in the 1/3 cup olive oil. Season with salt and pepper.

Without tearing the piquillo peppers, remove the seeds with your finger. In a small bowl, combine the goat cheese, finely chopped pecans, chives, parsley, and mashed garlic. Stuff the peppers with the seasoned goat cheese, dividing it evenly.

Core the tomatoes and cut them into large wedges or chunks. Put them in a large bowl and add the basil leaves, tearing them into smaller pieces. Add half of the dressing and toss well. Add the mixed lettuces and coarsely chopped pecans and toss again, adding more dressing as needed to coat the greens lightly. Taste for seasoning. Divide the tomato salad and the stuffed peppers among 6 large plates and serve immediately.

Enjoy with Cakebread Cellars Sauvignon Blanc or another young and crisp white wine.

Field Pea and Corn Salad

SERVES 6 TO 8

When Southerners like Birmingham chef Frank Stitt talk about field peas, they mean small shelling beans, such as black-eyed peas. (Crowder peas and lady peas also qualify, but they're less common.) When field peas are fresh, in summer, Chef Stitt, a 1999 Workshop attendee, shows them off in this salad, tossing them with grilled corn cut from the cob, tomato, grilled red onion, and herbs. Serve the salad when you're also grilling salmon, sausages, or pork chops, or with Brian's Grilled Mahimahi with Preserved Lemon Butter (page 113). If you can't find fresh black-eyed peas, use dried ones, soaked overnight, then simmered gently until tender.

2 ears fresh corn, unhusked

2 slices red onion, about 1/2 inch thick

2 tablespoons extra-virgin olive oil, plus more for brushing onion

1 cup cooked black-eyed peas

1/2 cup diced red tomato

1/2 cup diced green (unripe) tomato

1 small shallot, finely minced

2 tablespoons torn fresh basil leaves

2 tablespoons roughly chopped flat-leaf parsley

1 teaspoon red wine vinegar

1 teaspoon sherry vinegar

Kosher salt and freshly ground black pepper, to taste

Prepare a medium-hot charcoal fire or preheat a gas grill to high. Grill the corn, turning often, until the husks are charred in spots and the kernels undergo the color change that indicates that they are cooked, about 10 minutes. (Peel back the husks and check a few kernels to be sure.) When the corn is cool enough to handle, husk it and cut the kernels from the cob. Place them in a large mixing bowl.

Brush the onion slices lightly with olive oil on both sides. Grill the onion on both sides until charred in spots and lightly softened, about 5 minutes. Dice neatly and place in the bowl with the corn.

Add the remaining ingredients and toss gently. Let rest at room temperature for 1 hour, then serve.

Grilled Chicken Salad with Cherry Tomatoes, Avocado, and Tahini Dressing

SERVES 4

If you have ever made hummus, you probably still have a partial jar of tahini in your refrigerator. Here's one way to use more of it: in a creamy dressing for a grilled chicken salad. Brian seasons the chicken with *za'atar*, a Middle Eastern seasoning, and balances the tahini's faint bitterness with the sweetness of pine nuts to make the dish more wine friendly. You could substitute a meaty fish, such as mahimahi or tuna, for the chicken. That jar of tahini will be empty in no time. Note that the chicken needs to marinate for at least two hours.

3/4 pound skinless boneless chicken breasts

2 cloves garlic

Kosher salt

2 tablespoons extra-virgin olive oil

2 teaspoons freshly squeezed lemon juice

2 teaspoons *za'atar* (see Note)

TAHINI DRESSING

1/2 cup pine nuts

2 tablespoons tahini

1 small clove garlic, coarsely chopped

1/3 cup freshly squeezed lemon juice

1/4 cup extra-virgin olive oil

2 heads romaine hearts, broken into individual leaves

1 avocado, cut into large dice

1/2 pound cherry tomatoes, halved

2 tablespoons chopped fresh cilantro for garnish

Cut the chicken into 1-inch cubes. Make a paste of the garlic and 1/2 teaspoon salt by pounding in a mortar or mincing with a knife. Add the olive oil, lemon juice, and *za'atar*. Put the chicken in a bowl, add the oil mixture, and toss to coat. Cover and refrigerate for at least 2 hours or up to 12 hours.

For the dressing: Combine the pine nuts, tahini, garlic, lemon juice, olive oil, and 1/2 cup water in a blender. Blend until smooth. Season to taste with salt.

Prepare a medium-hot charcoal fire or preheat a gas grill to high.

Bring the chicken to room temperature. Thread on bamboo or metal skewers and season with salt.

If using bamboo skewers, prepare a doubled sheet of aluminum foil that you can position underneath the exposed ends of the skewers so they don't burn. Place the skewers on the grill so that the exposed ends rest over the foil. (If you are using metal skewers, you don't need to take this precaution.) Grill, turning as needed, until the chicken is firm to the touch, 6 to 7 minutes.

To serve, toss the romaine leaves with the dressing, using as much as you need to coat the leaves nicely. You may not need it all. Taste for salt. Arrange the romaine on a platter or on individual plates. Scatter the avocado and cherry tomatoes over the greens. Remove the chicken from the skewers and place the chicken on the greens. Garnish with the cilantro and serve immediately.

NOTE: *Za'atar* is a Middle Eastern seasoning that typically includes dried thyme, sesame seeds, and sumac. You can find it at well-stocked spice shops such as Whole Spice (see page 126) and stores catering to a Middle Eastern clientele.

Enjoy with Cakebread Cellars Sauvignon Blanc or another brisk white wine.

Squash Blossom Soup with Corn and Poblano Chiles

SERVES 8 TO 10

Chef Scott Neuman is a Latin cooking enthusiast who transformed the zucchini and corn in Dolores's garden into a lively chile-spiked soup during the 2009 Workshop. This recipe is an adaptation that goes well with Cakebread Cellars Chardonnay. The soup is light and bright, a distillation of early summer flavors and a delightful first course in warm weather.

2 pounds yellow pattypan squash or yellow zucchini

Kosher salt

1 large ear fresh corn, husked

2 poblano chiles

1 dozen large squash blossoms

2 tablespoons unsalted butter

2 small yellow onions, thinly sliced

1 quart chicken stock (page 190) or vegetable stock (page 191)

1 sprig fresh thyme

1/4 cup crème fraîche

1 small green zucchini, about 1/4 pound, cut into neat small dice

Freshly ground black pepper

Trim the ends of the pattypan squash or yellow zucchini. If using pattypan squash, cut them in half through the stem end. Slice the squash thinly. Put the slices in a colander or sieve set over a bowl. Add 2 teaspoons salt and toss well, then let stand for 20 minutes. Squeeze the squash vigorously, breaking up the slices with your hands to release their moisture. Drain well.

Cut the kernels from the corn cob. Cut the cob in half crosswise and reserve. Bring a medium pot of water to a boil over high heat and add the corn kernels. Blanch for 1 minute, then drain and chill quickly under cold running water.

Roast the chiles directly over a gas flame or under a broiler until blistered and charred on all sides. Let cool, then peel, seed, and dice.

Remove the papery squash blossoms from the stems and stamens and chop the blossoms coarsely.

Melt the butter in a large pot over moderate heat. Add the onions and sauté until softened, about 5 minutes. Add the drained yellow squash and toss to coat, then add the stock, thyme sprig, and reserved corn cob. Simmer gently, uncovered, for about 15 minutes. Remove the corn cob and the thyme sprig. Puree the soup in a blender, in batches, until as smooth as possible. Return to the pot and reheat gently. Whisk in the crème fraîche, the diced chiles, the blanched corn kernels, and the diced green zucchini. Season with salt and black pepper. Simmer gently for about 5 minutes to blend the flavors. Stir in the squash blossoms. If the soup is too thick for your taste, thin with water.

Enjoy with Cakebread Cellars Chardonnay or another Chardonnay with a silky texture.

Roasted Mushroom and Bacon Salad with Baby Greens and Sherry Vinaigrette

SERVES 6

Many Workshop chefs are unfamiliar with the clamshell mushrooms, maitake, and other exotic fungi that Gourmet Mushrooms cultivates (see page 84), so this company's table is always a magnet at our opening-day farmers' market. Chef George Brown, a 2006 participant, took advantage of the bounty to create a warm grilled mushroom and bacon salad. Although many people would be inclined to pair a red wine with a mushroom dish, we chose a mature Cakebread Cellars Chardonnay Reserve, which echoed all the earthy and smoky notes. In this adaptation of George's recipe, Brian has moved the preparation indoors for ease—first oven-roasting the mushrooms, then tossing them with browned cipolline onions, thick bacon, and tender greens. Serve at the first sign of autumn weather, followed with a pork roast or seared duck breasts.

3/4 pound cipolline onions

1 1/2 pounds mixed fresh mushrooms, such as trumpet, oyster, and shiitake

6 slices thick-cut applewood-smoked bacon, cut into 3/4-inch pieces

3 tablespoons extra-virgin olive oil

2 cloves garlic, minced

2 teaspoons minced fresh thyme

Kosher salt and freshly ground black pepper

SHERRY VINAIGRETTE

2 tablespoons sherry vinegar

1 large shallot, minced

1 teaspoon Dijon mustard

1/3 cup extra-virgin olive oil

6 ounces (about 6 handfuls) mixed lettuces

Preheat the oven to 450°F.

Trim off the root ends of the cipolline. Blanch them in boiling salted water for 30 seconds, then drain and chill quickly in ice water. Peel the cipolline (the skin should slip off easily) and cut in half.

Trim the ends of the trumpet mushrooms, then cut them in half lengthwise and crosswise. Remove the tough base of the oyster mushrooms and halve the caps if large. Cut off and discard the shiitake stems and quarter the caps.

In a large, ovenproof skillet, render the bacon over high heat until it begins to crisp, about 5 minutes. With a slotted spoon, scoop the bacon into a bowl; pour off the fat and discard.

Add the olive oil and onions to the skillet and sauté over high heat until lightly colored. Add the garlic and sauté briefly to release its fragrance. Add the mushrooms, thyme, salt to taste, and several grinds of black pepper. Toss well, then transfer the skillet to the oven. Roast until the mushrooms soften and begin to caramelize, about 20 minutes, tossing once or twice partway through. Remove from the oven and add the bacon. Let cool to room temperature.

For the sherry vinaigrette: In a small bowl, whisk together the vinegar, shallot, and mustard. Gradually whisk in the olive oil. Season to taste with salt and pepper.

Put the greens in a large bowl and add the cooled mushrooms, onions, and bacon. Add enough vinaigrette to coat the salad lightly and toss gently. Taste for seasoning, then serve immediately.

Enjoy with a mature Cakebread Cellars Chardonnay Reserve or another rich white wine with some age.

Autumn Squash Soup with Puff Pastry

SERVES 6

By adding a puff pastry top, Chef Albert Bouchard transforms an easy autumn vegetable soup into a first course suitable for company. The puff pastry seals in all the aromas until diners breach the flaky caps with their spoons. Note that you will need individual ovenproof soup crocks, similar to the type used for French onion soup. The diameter on top should be no more than 5 inches to have the proper ratio of soup to pastry. Chef Bouchard attended the 2006 Workshop.

1/2 acorn squash (about 3/4 pound), seeded

1 large orange-fleshed sweet potato, such as a Garnet yam (about 3/4 pound)

2 tablespoons unsalted butter

1 yellow onion, halved and thinly sliced

1/3 cup brandy

1/2 teaspoon ground ginger

1/4 teaspoon ground cinnamon

1 quart chicken stock (page 190) or vegetable stock (page 191), plus more as needed

1/4 cup heavy cream

Kosher salt and freshly ground black pepper

1/2 pound frozen puff pastry, thawed but cold

Egg wash: 1 whole egg beaten with 1 tablespoon milk

Preheat the oven to 400°F. Place the squash half, cut side down, in a pie tin or small baking dish with 1/2 inch of water. Bake, uncovered, until the flesh can be easily pierced with the tip of a paring knife, about 40 minutes, adding a little more water if necessary. When cool, scoop the flesh out of the skin. You should have about 1 cup.

Pierce the sweet potato in several places with a fork. Place it in a pie tin or on a baking sheet and bake alongside the squash until tender when pierced, about 1 hour. When cool enough to handle, scoop the flesh out of the skin. You should have about 1 cup.

Melt the butter in a large pot over medium heat. Add the onion and sauté until soft, about 5 minutes. Add the brandy and simmer for 1 to 2 minutes to burn off the alcohol. Add the squash, sweet potato, ginger, cinnamon, and stock. Bring to a simmer and cook gently for about 5 minutes to blend the flavors.

In a blender or food processor, puree the contents of the pot until smooth. Pour into a clean pot. Whisk in the cream. Thin with additional stock if needed to achieve a pleasing soup consistency. Season to taste with salt and pepper. Let cool to room temperature.

Preheat the oven to 425°F. On a lightly floured work surface, roll the puff pastry to a 1/8-inch thickness. Cut 6 rounds, each 2 inches larger in diameter than the top of the soup bowl (for a 5-inch bowl, cut a 7-inch round). To guide you, invert a bowl onto the flattened pastry and cut around it. You can gather and reroll the scraps once. Put the rounds on a baking sheet and refrigerate for 20 minutes.

Divide the soup among 6 ovenproof bowls. Brush the rim of each bowl with egg wash. Cover with a round of pastry and press the pastry firmly around the sides so the top is taut, like a drum. Make sure there are no cracks in the pastry. Brush the tops lightly with egg wash.

Bake until the pastry is puffed and golden brown, about 25 minutes. Serve immediately.

Enjoy with Cakebread Cellars Chardonnay Reserve or another full-bodied, oak-aged white wine.

Haricots Verts and Pear Salad with Hazelnuts and Prosciutto

SERVES 6

Because of their tart dressings, salads are not always wine-friendly dishes, but adding cured meat like prosciutto can bridge the divide. Toasted nuts help, too, contributing a buttery note that mellows vinegar's sharpness. This autumn salad from the winery pairs slender French *haricots verts* (green beans) with a blend of cool-weather greens and a hazelnut-oil dressing. Follow it with roast chicken or duck.

1/2 pound *haricots verts*

VINAIGRETTE

2 tablespoons cider vinegar

1 small shallot, minced

1 teaspoon Dijon mustard

3 tablespoons hazelnut oil

3 tablespoons extra-virgin olive oil

Kosher salt and freshly ground black pepper

1 head frisée

2 small Belgian endives

1 ounce (about 1 handful) arugula

1/4 cup coarsely chopped toasted hazelnuts

1 Bartlett pear, ripe but firm

8 to 12 thin slices prosciutto di Parma

Trim the ends of the *haricots verts*. Bring a large pot of salted water to a boil over high heat. Cook the beans until crisp-tender, 2 to 4 minutes, then drain and transfer to ice water to preserve the color. Drain again and pat dry. Cut in half crosswise. Place in a large mixing bowl.

For the vinaigrette: Put the vinegar, shallot, and mustard in a small bowl and whisk to blend. Gradually whisk in the oils. Season with salt and pepper.

Trim the core and any dark green outer leaves and leaf tips from the frisée. Tear the pale yellow center leaves into bite-size pieces. Slice the endives on a slight diagonal into 1-inch pieces. Separate into individual layers and discard the core. Add the frisée, endive, arugula, and hazelnuts to the bowl with the beans.

Cut the pear in half, remove the core and slice thinly lengthwise. Add to the bowl. Toss with enough of the vinaigrette to coat the salad lightly; you may not need it all.

If the prosciutto slices are large, tear in half. Make a loose ring of prosciutto on each plate, then mound a handful of salad in the center of the ring. Serve immediately.

Enjoy with Cakebread Cellars Chardonnay Reserve or another full-bodied white wine.

Indian Lentil Soup

SERVES 10

As Cakebread Cellars expanded sales overseas, we began inviting chefs from abroad to participate in the Workshop. Predictably, some new and intriguing scents soon emerged from our kitchen. This warmly spiced lentil soup is Brian's invention, but he devised it after working with Indian chef Sujan Mukherjee at the 2008 Workshop and observing his spicing. Now Brian makes this wholesome soup with the Napa elementary school students that he teaches regularly, and he demonstrates the recipe at our employees' wellness classes.

1 pound red lentils (see Note)

3 tablespoons extra-virgin olive oil

1 small yellow onion, minced

1 celery rib, minced

2 cloves garlic, minced

1 serrano chile, seeded and minced

1 teaspoon sweet paprika

1/2 teaspoon ground cumin

1/4 teaspoon ground turmeric

1 1/2 cups peeled, seeded, and chopped plum tomato (fresh or canned)

1 bay leaf

Kosher salt

2 tablespoons chopped cilantro, plus more for garnish

1 teaspoon *garam masala* (Indian spice blend)

Put the lentils in a large pot and cover with cold water. Swish with your hand to release surface starch, then pour off the water. Repeat this rinsing and draining until the water runs clear.

Cover the lentils with 2 quarts cold water. Bring to a simmer over medium heat, skimming any foam. Reduce the heat to maintain a gentle simmer and cook, uncovered, until the lentils are tender and beginning to fall apart, about 15 minutes.

In another large pot, warm the olive oil over medium heat. Add the onion, celery, garlic, chile, paprika, cumin, and turmeric and sauté until the vegetables are soft, about 10 minutes. Add the tomato and bay leaf and cook, stirring, until the tomato softens and the juices thicken, about 5 minutes. Stir in the cooked lentils and their liquid. Add 1 tablespoon salt. Simmer for 10 minutes, then stir in the cilantro and *garam masala* and taste for salt. Simmer for 5 minutes to blend the flavors. Serve immediately, garnishing each portion with a little additional chopped cilantro.

NOTE: Red lentils are available at Indian markets, natural foods stores, and some well-stocked supermarkets. Despite the name, they are closer to salmon-pink in color.

Enjoy with Cakebread Cellars Napa Valley Chardonnay or another barrel-fermented Chardonnay.

Quinoa, Golden Beet, and Orange Salad

SERVES 6

Brian does most of the cooking at home for his wife, Kristina, and their two small children, but this salad is one of Kristina's specialties. She adapts it to the season, but quinoa is always the starting point. Nutty and quick cooking, quinoa is high in protein and will hold up for about an hour after it's dressed. Serve this refreshing winter salad with pork, chicken, or fish, or with feta for a meatless meal.

8 golden beets, golf ball size

1 1/2 cups quinoa

2 large navel oranges

1/2 cup thinly sliced scallions, white and green parts

3/4 cup coarsely chopped toasted walnuts

DRESSING

3 tablespoons sherry vinegar

2 teaspoons Dijon mustard

1 teaspoon honey

2 tablespoons walnut oil

2 tablespoons extra-virgin olive oil

Kosher salt and freshly ground black pepper

Preheat the oven to 400°F. Wrap the beets in a loose aluminum-foil package, sealing the package tightly. Bake until the beets are tender when pierced with the tip of a paring knife, 45 minutes to 1 hour. When cool enough to handle, peel the beets and cut into 3/4-inch dice.

Bring a large pot of salted water to a boil over high heat. Add the quinoa and cook until tender, about 12 minutes. Drain and spread on a sheet pan to cool.

Cut a slice off both ends of each orange so they will stand upright. Stand each orange on a work surface and, using a sharp knife, remove all the peel and membrane by slicing from top to bottom all the way around the orange, following the contour of the fruit. Cut the oranges into 3/4-inch cubes.

Put the cooled quinoa in a large bowl. Add the beets, oranges, scallions, and walnuts.

For the dressing: In a small bowl, whisk together the vinegar, mustard, and honey. Gradually whisk in the oils. Season with salt and pepper. Add to the salad and toss to coat. Taste, adjust the seasoning, and serve.

Sweet Potato and Chicory Salad

SERVES 6 TO 8

For this salad, Brian likes to mix the moist, orange-fleshed sweet potatoes—such as Garnet or Jewel—with drier, yellow-fleshed varieties. Ask your produce merchant to point you to the right types if you aren't sure. After roasting and cubing the sweet potatoes, Brian tosses them with a mix of bitter chicories, a nutty sherry vinaigrette, and fine shavings of sheep's milk cheese—an inspired marriage of contrasting textures and flavors. Serve with pork chops or a pork roast for a winter dinner.

2 pounds sweet potatoes, preferably both yellow-fleshed and orange-fleshed varieties

1 head radicchio

1 small head frisée

2 Belgian endives

Sherry vinaigrette (page 67)

3 ounces Bellwether Farms San Andreas or other aged sheep's milk cheese, in one piece

Preheat the oven to 400°F. Pierce the sweet potatoes in several places with a fork, place on a baking sheet, and roast until they are tender when pierced, about 1 hour. Let cool, peel, and cut into 3/4-inch chunks.

Cut the radicchio in half, cut away the core, then tear the leaves into bite-size pieces and place in a salad bowl.

Trim the core and any dark green outer leaves and leaf tips from the frisée. Tear the pale yellow center leaves into bite-size pieces. Cut the endive crosswise into 1-inch rounds. Add the frisée and endive to the salad bowl and toss to mix.

Add enough of the vinaigrette to coat the salad lightly (you may not need it all) and toss well. Add the sweet potatoes and toss again gently. Taste for seasoning. Divide the salad among salad plates. With a vegetable peeler or cheese plane, shave cheese over each portion, dividing it evenly. Serve immediately.

Enjoy with Cakebread Cellars Sauvignon Blanc or another dry white wine with good acidity.

SANDWICHES AND PIZZAS

SPRING

SUMMER

FALL

WINTER

Pizza with Asparagus, Spring Onions, Pancetta, and Ricotta

MAKES FOUR 8-INCH PIZZAS

In late spring, when California asparagus are still available and the Cakebread garden is yielding the year's first onions, Brian makes this delicate pizza *bianca* (a "white pizza," or pizza without tomato sauce). The fresh-dug onions haven't been cured yet, so they don't have papery skins, and their flavor is mild. Many supermarkets sell "spring onions" that look like thick scallions with a bulbous root end. They would work in this recipe, as would leeks or even cured yellow onions, but uncured onions have the most delicate taste. Choose a fresh ricotta without pectin or other stabilizers. The Bellwether Farms ricotta from neighboring Sonoma County is our favorite.

1 1/2 tablespoons extra-virgin olive oil

6 cups thinly sliced spring onions or yellow onions

Kosher salt

1 pound asparagus

1 pound whole-milk ricotta cheese

Freshly ground white pepper

Pizza dough (page 192)

Cornmeal or durum flour for dusting

4 tablespoons freshly grated Parmesan cheese

20 paper-thin slices (4 to 5 ounces) pancetta, in coiled rounds

Heat a large, wide-bottomed pot over medium heat. Add the olive oil, onions, and a large pinch of salt. Cook until the onions are soft, about 30 minutes, stirring occasionally and lowering the heat if needed to keep them from browning. Let cool.

Snap off the woody ends of the asparagus. Slice the trimmed spears on the diagonal about 1/4 inch thick.

Bring a pot of salted water to a boil over high heat. Add the asparagus and cook until tender, 1 to 2 minutes. Drain and rinse with cold water to chill quickly. Pat dry.

Season the ricotta with salt and white pepper.

At least 45 minutes before baking, put a pizza stone on the bottom rack of the oven and preheat the oven to its highest setting (500°F to 550°F).

With lightly floured fingers, flatten a ball of pizza dough into a round on a lightly floured work surface. Pick up the round with both hands and, grasping the round by an edge, rotate the dough clockwise between your fingertips, always holding it by the edge. As you rotate the dough, stretch it into an 8-inch circle; the dough will also stretch and lengthen from its own weight. Alternatively, drape the flattened round over your lightly floured knuckles and rotate the dough, moving your knuckles slightly farther apart, until the round stretches into an 8-inch circle.

Place on a pizza peel lightly dusted with cornmeal or durum flour. Work quickly now to prevent sticking.

Using one-quarter of the onion mixture, spread it evenly over the surface of the dough. Scatter asparagus over the onions, using one-quarter of the total. Dollop one-quarter (4 ounces) of the ricotta on the pizza in 7 to 8 mounds. Sprinkle with 1 tablespoon Parmesan. Arrange 5 pancetta slices, still coiled in rounds, on top, spacing them evenly.

Slide the pizza onto the pizza stone and bake until the crust is brown and crisp, 8 to 10 minutes. Remove from the oven. Cut into slices and serve hot. Repeat with the remaining three balls of dough and the remaining topping.

Enjoy with Cakebread Cellars Sauvignon Blanc or another lean and refreshing white wine.

Just a Few Sheep

CINDY CALLAHAN, a former nurse, wanted just a few sheep to control the grasses around her rural Sonoma County home. But that purchase, in the mid-1980s, evolved into Bellwether Farms, an artisan producer of fresh and aged cheeses from cow's and sheep's milk.

Cindy's son, Liam, now handles most of the cheesemaking, and at Cakebread Cellars, we use almost everything he makes. His aged cheeses—the cow's milk Carmody and sheep's milk San Andreas and peppercorn-studded Pepato—find their way onto our cheese boards. The Crescenza, a soft and supple cow's milk square, melts into luscious puddles on pizza. Brian uses Bellwether Farms crème fraîche in creamy salad dressings with chopped garden herbs and stuffs mushroom caps with the dairy's fromage blanc. Sometimes, for the late breakfast on the last day of the Work-

shop, Brian will spread toasts with Bellwether Farms fromage blanc, top them with sliced fresh figs, pop the toasts under the broiler, and then drizzle them with Marshall Farms honey.

Bellwether's exquisite Old World–style basket ricotta—made with cow's milk and, on a smaller scale, with sheep's milk—always seduces chefs at the farmers' market that opens the Workshop. Cindy stands behind the table, offering samples of made-that-morning ricotta drizzled with extra-virgin olive oil, and people can't get enough. Cakebread resident chef Tom Sixsmith sometimes spoons the sheep's milk ricotta on bruschetta and tops it with sautéed mushrooms for an hors d'oeuvre to complement our Chardonnay. And the company's rich sheep's milk yogurt is a winery staff favorite. We always have some in the kitchen refrigerator, just for us.

Soft Tacos with Chipotle-Braised Rabbit, Black Beans, and Pickled Cabbage

SERVES 8

On the first morning of the Workshop, participants rise early to pick grapes before the temperature soars. These chefs may labor in hot kitchens every day, but on grape-harvest day, they learn what real work is like. By midday, they are famished. We keep lunch casual, knowing that a big dinner will follow. Typically, we serve Mexican food, like these soft tacos, with from-scratch tortillas prepared outdoors on a *comal* (Mexican griddle) by winery staffers Brenda Godinez and Virginia Barrera. Rubaiyat, a blend of red varieties, is perfect for the occasion. Note that the beans need to soak overnight.

1/2 pound dried black beans

Kosher salt

4-pound fresh rabbit or chicken, cut into 8 pieces

Freshly ground black pepper

3 tablespoons extra-virgin olive oil

1 yellow onion, minced

2 cloves garlic, minced

1 1/2 cups peeled, seeded, and diced tomatoes (fresh or canned)

1/2 cup Cakebread Cellars Sauvignon Blanc

2 canned chipotle chiles in adobo, seeded and minced

2 bay leaves

PICKLED CABBAGE

1/4 head cabbage, cored and sliced very thinly

1 large carrot, coarsely grated

1/2 cup minced red onion

1 teaspoon sugar

2 tablespoons cider vinegar

3 tablespoons vegetable oil

1 serrano chile, halved lengthwise

16 corn tortillas, warmed

1/4 cup chopped cilantro

Lime wedges for serving

In a large pot, soak the black beans overnight in water to cover by 2 inches. The next day, add more water as needed to cover the beans by 2 inches. Bring to a boil over high heat, then adjust the heat to maintain a gentle simmer and cook until the beans are tender, about 1 hour. Add 2 teaspoons salt and let cool in the liquid.

Preheat the oven to 350°F. Season the rabbit all over with salt and pepper. Heat a wide, deep ovenproof pot over high heat. Add the olive oil and sear the meat on all sides until lightly browned, about 5 minutes. Transfer the meat to a platter and set aside. Add the onion and sauté until soft, about 5 minutes. Add the garlic and sauté briefly to release its fragrance.

Add the tomatoes, wine, chipotle chiles, and bay leaves. Bring to a simmer and return the meat to the pot. Cover tightly and place in the middle of the oven. Cook until the rabbit is fork-tender, about 1 1/2 hours, turning the pieces over halfway through. Remove the pot from the oven and let the meat cool to room temperature. Pull the meat from the bones and shred by hand. Return the meat to the pot and toss with the sauce. Taste for seasoning.

For the pickled cabbage: Toss the cabbage, carrot, and red onion with 1 teaspoon salt in a colander; let drain for about 20 minutes to wilt slightly. Squeeze the vegetables to remove excess moisture, then transfer to a bowl and toss with the sugar and vinegar.

Drain the beans, reserving the liquid. Heat the vegetable oil in a medium saucepan over medium heat. Add the serrano chile and sauté for about 1 minute to release its flavor. Set the chile aside if you prefer the beans relatively mild; leave it in if you prefer them spicy. Add the beans and 1 cup of the reserved cooking liquid. Bring to a simmer while mashing with a potato masher until the beans are nearly smooth. Simmer for about 5 minutes to blend the flavors, thinning with reserved bean liquid if needed and stirring to prevent scorching. If the beans are too thin, simmer until they are as thick as you like. Taste for salt and keep warm.

To serve, reheat the rabbit if necessary. Spread a large tablespoon of the refried beans on each tortilla. Top with a generous spoonful of the braised rabbit, some pickled cabbage, and chopped cilantro. Arrange the tacos on a platter or individual plates and accompany with lime wedges.

Enjoy with Cakebread Cellars Rubaiyat or another young and fruity red wine.

Rabbit Raised Right

CHEFS IN THE SAN FRANCISCO BAY AREA are fortunate to have a network of suppliers who practice sustainable agriculture and humane livestock production. These suppliers often know each other, so one will lead you to another. That's how we found Mark Pasternak, who raises rabbits for meat on his Devil's Gulch Ranch in Marin County. He and his wife, Miriam, a veterinarian, also grow wine grapes and raise other livestock, but they are building a reputation among local chefs for the quality of their rabbit. Even in the well-supplied Bay Area, fresh rabbit raised humanely can be hard to find.

At Devil's Gulch Ranch, each rabbit has its own spacious cage and a diet free of hormones and antibiotics. The Pasternaks breed for quality meat, not just for fast growth. They use a wind turbine to produce some of the ranch power, host summer camps and after-school programs for kids, and work as volunteers in Haiti to develop a meat-rabbit industry there. We love supporting a business with these ambitions and ideals.

Workshop chefs typically separate the rabbit into parts: the loins, which are suited to roasting; and the fore legs and hind legs, which are better for braising. Canadian chef Jonathan Gushue made rabbit rillettes during the 2008 Workshop. Brian's chipotle-braised rabbit (opposite page), served in soft tacos or on crisp tostadas, shows this tender, lean meat at its best.

Grilled Summer Vegetable Sandwich with Romesco Sauce and Serrano Ham

SERVES 4

Save this pressed sandwich for the height of summer, when you can get locally grown zucchini, eggplant, and tomatoes. After grilling the zucchini and eggplant, layer them on a roll slathered with romesco, the Spanish tomato and almond sauce. (Refrigerate any unused romesco and use it within a day or two on another sandwich or with grilled fish or shrimp.) The sandwich can be made hours ahead, so it's a good choice for a backpack lunch or a picnic. Omit the ham to make it vegetarian. Piquillo peppers are small, slightly spicy roasted red peppers sold in jars at shops that specialize in Spanish or Mediterranean foods (see Ingredient Resources, page 193).

ROMESCO SAUCE

1 dried ancho (pasilla) chile, stemmed and seeded

1/2 cup extra-virgin olive oil

1 slice dense, day-old Italian-style bread, about 6 by 3 inches and 3/4 inch thick, crust removed

3 large cloves garlic, peeled

1/2 cup canned plum tomato (pulp only, no puree)

1/3 cup marcona almonds (see Notes, page 41)

1 tablespoon red wine vinegar

Kosher salt

1 globe eggplant (about 1 1/4 pounds)

1 small zucchini (about 3/4 pound)

2 small cloves garlic

Kosher salt

1/2 cup extra-virgin olive oil

1 tablespoon chopped fresh thyme

Freshly ground black pepper

4 sandwich rolls, 5 to 6 inches long

Romesco sauce (recipe follows)

4 ounces (4 handfuls) arugula

8 thin slices Spanish serrano ham

8 piquillo peppers, slit opened and seeded, or 2 large red bell peppers, roasted, peeled, seeded, and sliced

For the romesco sauce: In a small bowl, cover the chile with hot water and let soak for 15 minutes to soften. Drain and tear into 3 or 4 pieces.

In a small skillet, warm the olive oil over medium heat. Add the bread and fry until golden-brown and crisp on both sides, about 30 seconds per side. Transfer with tongs to a plate and let cool. Reduce the heat to medium-low, add the garlic cloves, and fry until golden all over, about 1 minute. Transfer with tongs to the plate with the bread. Let the oil cool, then transfer it to a measuring cup with a pour spout.

In a food processor, combine the bread (breaking it into smaller pieces to fit), garlic, chile, tomato, almonds, and vinegar. Puree until smooth, scraping down the sides of the bowl once or twice. With the machine running, add the reserved olive oil in a slow, steady stream to emulsify, as if making mayonnaise. Transfer to a bowl and stir in salt to taste.

Prepare a hot charcoal fire or preheat a gas grill to high. Trim the ends of the eggplant, peel it, and slice crosswise 1/4 to 1/3 inch thick. Trim the ends of the zucchini and slice lengthwise as thickly as the eggplant.

In a mortar, pound the garlic to a paste with a pinch of salt, or mince garlic and salt to a paste with a knife. Combine the garlic paste, olive oil, and thyme in a small bowl. Brush the eggplant and zucchini on both sides with the olive oil mixture and season with salt and pepper. Grill on both sides until lightly charred and soft, about 2 minutes per side for both vegetables. Let cool to room temperature.

continued on next page

Cut the sandwich rolls in half and pull out some of the soft interior crumb. Spread each side with 2 tablespoons romesco sauce. On each of the four bottom halves, make a layer of arugula, then 2 slices serrano ham, some of the grilled eggplant, piquillo peppers, and grilled zucchini. Top with the upper half of the roll. Press the sandwiches for 20 minutes between two plates or sheet pans with a couple of 2-pound weights on top. Cut in half on the diagonal and serve.

Enjoy with Cakebread Cellars Rubaiyat or other youthful, fruity red wine.

Grilled Pizza with Summer Squash, Cherry Tomatoes, and Fresh Mozzarella

MAKES FOUR 8-INCH PIZZAS

It takes a little more attention to grill a pizza than to bake one, but the smoky touch of the grill is appealing—the next best thing to baking in a wood-fired oven. When Brian teaches pizza classes at the winery in summer, he demonstrates the grilling technique because so few people have a wood oven at home. The trick is to start the pizza crust in a hot zone to set it, and then flip it and move it to a cooler zone to add the topping and finish cooking. This topping is vegetarian, but you could add some crumbled sausage or pancetta, if you like.

TOMATO SAUCE

2 tablespoons extra-virgin olive oil

2 large cloves garlic, minced

Pinch of red chile flakes

1½ pounds ripe plum tomatoes, peeled, seeded, and diced

1 sprig fresh basil

Kosher salt

2 tablespoons extra-virgin olive oil, plus more for brushing the dough

1 pound summer squash, preferably green and yellow varieties, cut into ½-inch dice

2 cloves garlic, minced

1 tablespoon chopped flat-leaf parsley

1 tablespoon chopped fresh basil, plus a few more leaves for garnish

Pizza dough (page 192)

1 pint cherry tomatoes, halved

½ pound fresh whole-milk mozzarella, coarsely grated

4 tablespoons freshly grated Parmesan cheese

Freshly ground black pepper

For the tomato sauce: Heat the oil in a skillet over high heat. Add the garlic and chile flakes and sauté until fragrant, about 30 seconds. Add the tomatoes and basil. Season with salt and simmer briskly, stirring often, until the tomatoes collapse into a thick sauce, about 10 minutes. Remove the basil sprig and remove the sauce from the heat.

In a large skillet over high heat, warm the 2 tablespoons olive oil. Add the diced squash and a pinch of salt and sauté until slightly softened, about 2 minutes. Add the garlic, parsley, and basil and sauté until fragrant, 1 to 2 minutes. Spread the mixture on a baking sheet to cool.

Prepare a medium-hot charcoal fire, then move the coals to one half of the grill, arranging them in an evenly thick layer. Or preheat a gas grill, turning one burner to high and one to medium.

With lightly floured fingers on a lightly floured work surface, flatten one ball of pizza dough into a round. Pick up the round with both hands and, grasping the round by an edge, rotate the dough clockwise between your fingertips, always holding it by the edge. As you rotate the dough, stretch it into an 8-inch circle; the dough will also stretch and lengthen from its own weight. Alternatively, drape the flattened round over your lightly floured knuckles and rotate the dough, moving your knuckles slightly farther apart, until the round stretches into an 8-inch circle.

Set the stretched dough on the floured work surface. Brush the top with olive oil, then place the dough directly over the coals or on the hot side of the gas grill, oiled side down. Brush the new top side with olive oil. Cook until the underside is nicely marked by

continued on next page

the grill and the dough is firm enough to move with tongs, about 1 minute. Give the dough a quarter turn and continue cooking for about 1 minute longer, using tongs to check the bottom often to be sure it is not burning.

With tongs, flip the pizza over onto the grill's cooler zone. Working quickly, brush with one-quarter of the tomato sauce, spreading it evenly but leaving a 1/2-inch border uncovered. Top with one-quarter of the squash, cherry tomatoes, and mozzarella, in that order. Sprinkle with 1 tablespoon Parmesan and a few grinds of pepper. Cover the grill and cook until the mozzarella melts, about 2 minutes.

Transfer the pizza to a cutting board. Sprinkle with a few torn basil leaves. Cut into wedges and serve immediately. Repeat with the remaining 3 balls of dough.

Enjoy with Cakebread Cellars Sauvignon Blanc or another refreshing white wine.

Flawless Fungus

THE IMPECCABLE FUNGI from Gourmet Mushrooms enhance Cakebread Cellars menus year round. Unlike wild mushrooms, which emerge only when conditions are right and can be weather-beaten by the time foragers find them, Gourmet Mushrooms arrive at the winery in pristine condition. They mature in a sawdust-based medium in a controlled environment, a setting that challenges any conventional notion of farming. Entering a room lined with shelves of fungi sprouting from bottles feels like a scene out of science fiction. When we take Workshop chefs to visit the production facility in Sonoma County, they are captivated by this convergence of science and nature.

When Malcolm Clark founded Gourmet Mushrooms in 1977, fresh shiitake were exotic. The company was the first in the Western Hemisphere to grow them commercially. Now they have abandoned shiitake—they are far too common—in favor of a half-dozen more unusual types, like maitake (hen-of-the-woods) and Alba Clamshell (known in Japan as *hon-shimeji* or *buna-shimeji*).

Gourmet Mushrooms has participated in the Workshop every year since the beginning, and we have enjoyed watching the company's product line grow. Brian particularly likes the Trumpet Royale, a large, thick-stemmed, meaty mushroom that he often roasts in our wood-burning oven. But many Workshop chefs like to mix varieties to showcase the contrasting colors and textures, as chef George Brown did in his Roasted Mushroom and Bacon Salad (page 67).

Pizza with Cremini Mushrooms, New Potatoes, and Crescenza Cheese

MAKES FOUR 8-INCH PIZZAS

Brian spreads a roasted-garlic paste on the dough under the mushrooms and potatoes, which gives this pizza an irresistible fragrance. If you have access to wild mushrooms, by all means use them. Bellwether Farms Crescenza cheese is a soft, supple, young cow's milk cheese that melts well; mozzarella is stretchier, but a good substitute.

1 whole head garlic

5 tablespoons plus 1 teaspoon extra-virgin olive oil, plus more for brushing

4 small fingerling potatoes, very thinly sliced (no need to peel)

1 pound cremini (common brown) mushrooms, ends trimmed, sliced

2 cloves garlic, minced

Kosher salt and freshly ground black pepper

Pizza dough (page 192)

Cornmeal or durum flour for dusting

1/2 pound Bellwether Farms Crescenza cheese or fresh whole-milk mozzarella

4 tablespoons freshly grated Parmesan cheese

4 small handfuls arugula

Preheat the oven to 400°F. Slice about 1/4 inch off the stem end (opposite the root end) of the garlic head to expose the individual cloves. Put the whole garlic head, root end down, on a sheet of aluminum foil and drizzle with 1 teaspoon olive oil. Seal the foil package and place in the oven until the cloves are soft, 45 to 50 minutes. (You will have to open the package to check.) Let cool. Squeeze the softened garlic cloves out of the papery skins and mash with 2 tablespoons olive oil into a paste.

Bring a small pot of salted water to a boil over high heat. Add the potatoes and cook until just tender, about 3 minutes. Drain.

Heat a large skillet over high heat. Add the remaining 3 tablespoons olive oil. When the oil is hot, add the mushrooms and sauté until well browned, about 5 minutes. Add the minced garlic and season with salt and pepper. Cook, stirring, for 1 to 2 minutes longer to release the garlic fragrance.

At least 45 minutes before baking, put a pizza stone on a rack in the bottom third of the oven and preheat the oven to its highest setting (500°F to 550°F).

With lightly floured fingers on a lightly floured work surface, flatten a ball of pizza dough into a round. Pick up the round with both hands and, grasping the round by an edge, rotate the dough clockwise between your fingertips, always holding it by the edge. As you rotate the dough, stretch it into an 8-inch circle; the dough will also stretch and lengthen from its own weight. Alternatively, drape the flattened round over your lightly floured knuckles and rotate the dough, moving your knuckles slightly farther apart, until the round stretches into an 8-inch circle. Place the dough on a pizza peel lightly dusted with cornmeal or durum flour. Work quickly now to prevent sticking.

continued on next page

Brush the dough with one-quarter of the garlic paste. Top with one-quarter of the potato slices, then scatter with one-quarter of the mushrooms. Distribute the Crescenza cheese in 5 or 6 clumps, using a total of 2 ounces. Sprinkle with 1 tablespoon Parmesan. Slide onto the pizza stone and bake until the crust is brown and crisp, about 10 minutes.

Transfer the pizza to a cutting board and scatter a handful of arugula over the surface. Cut into wedges and serve immediately. Repeat with the remaining 3 balls of dough.

Enjoy with Cakebread Cellars Chardonnay or another rich, barrel-fermented Chardonnay.

Narsai's Wheat Berry and Flax Bread

MAKES TWO LOAVES, 1¼ TO 1½ POUNDS EACH

Narsai David, a San Francisco Bay Area radio personality and former restaurateur, joined us at the Workshop for many years as a sort of camp counselor. He would lead the chefs in their brainstorming sessions, and while the chefs worked feverishly on their courses, he would co-opt one quiet corner of the kitchen to make bread. Narsai surprised us every year with imaginative loaves that almost always incorporated whole grains, like the brown rice from California's Lundberg Family Farms, or this three-seeded bread that he devised after sampling a similar bread in Australia.

⅓ cup whole wheat berries

⅓ cup flax seeds

4 cups all-purpose flour, plus more for kneading

1 cup whole-wheat flour

1 package (¼ ounce) active dry yeast

1½ teaspoons kosher salt

2 cups lukewarm water

2 tablespoons vegetable oil

2 tablespoons molasses

¼ cup sesame seeds

Put the wheat berries in a small saucepan with water to cover by 2 inches. Bring to a simmer and cook until tender, about 1 hour. Drain and let cool.

Toast the flax seeds in a small dry skillet over moderately high heat, shaking constantly, until the seeds darken and develop a toasty aroma. Be careful; they jump like popcorn when they get hot.

In a large bowl, combine the all-purpose flour, whole-wheat flour, yeast, and salt. Mix to blend. Stir in the wheat berries and flax seeds, then add the water, oil, and molasses. Stir until the dough comes together, then turn it out onto a work surface and knead until smooth and elastic, about 5 minutes, adding all-purpose flour as necessary to prevent sticking.

Transfer the dough to a lightly oiled bowl and turn to coat with oil. Cover the bowl with plastic wrap and set it in a warm, draft-free place until the dough doubles, 1 to 1½ hours.

Put the sesame seeds in a bowl. Turn the dough out on a floured board, punch it down, and divide it in half. Shape each half into a round. Moisten the surface with a wet towel or a spray bottle of water, then dip the surface of the bread in the sesame seeds.

Place the loaves on a baking sheet dusted with cornmeal or lined with parchment paper. Cover the loaves with a dish towel and let them rise in a warm, draft-free place until almost doubled, about 1 hour.

Preheat the oven to 400°F. Place a rack in the middle of the oven.

With a razor blade, cut 4 deep gashes in the shape of a large square on the surface of each loaf. Cover the loaves again and let rise for another 10 to 15 minutes.

Place the loaves in the oven and mist them well with water from a spray bottle. Repeat the misting two more times at 10-minute intervals. Bake until the surface is well browned, the crust is firm, and the loaves sound hollow when rapped on the bottom with your knuckle, about 45 minutes. Cool completely on a rack before slicing.

Grilled Red Hawk Cheese Sandwich with Pickled Red Cabbage

SERVES 4

This modern interpretation of a comfort-food classic comes from chef Tom Wolfe, who participated in the 2004 Workshop. Chef Wolfe uses the pungent washed-rind Red Hawk, a cheese from California's Cowgirl Creamery (see page 177), but you can substitute another washed-rind cheese such as French Époisses or a milder Havarti. The pickled red cabbage provides a crunchy counterpoint to the oozy melted cheese. You will have more pickled cabbage than you need for the sandwiches, but it keeps well. Use it on a hamburger or meatloaf sandwich, or as a slaw.

PICKLED CABBAGE

1/4 head (about 3/4 pound) red cabbage, cored and finely sliced

2 tablespoons kosher salt

1 1/2 tablespoons Champagne vinegar

1 tablespoon extra-virgin olive oil

1 teaspoon sugar

1/4 teaspoon celery seeds

4 teaspoons Dijon mustard

8 slices brioche from a sandwich loaf, about 1/3 inch thick

1/4 pound Cowgirl Creamery Red Hawk, or other semisoft washed-rind cheese

2 tablespoons unsalted butter, or more as needed

For the pickled cabbage: Toss the cabbage with the salt in a colander and set aside to wilt for 30 minutes. Rinse the cabbage thoroughly, then taste to be sure the rinsed cabbage is not too salty (if it is, rinse again). Squeeze well to remove excess moisture.

In a nonreactive bowl, combine the wilted cabbage, vinegar, olive oil, sugar, and celery seed. Mix well.

To assemble the sandwiches, spread Dijon mustard over 4 slices of bread, using about 1 teaspoon per slice.

Lay the 4 slices of bread, mustard side up, on the work surface. Top each with 1/4 cup of the cabbage, then with 1 ounce of cheese in 2 or 3 slices. Top with the second slice of bread and press lightly.

Melt 1 tablespoon butter in a 10-inch nonstick skillet over moderate heat. Add 2 sandwiches to the pan and cook until browned, about 2 minutes, then turn and cook until the second side is browned and the cheese is molten, about 2 minutes longer. Cut each sandwich in half on the diagonal and serve immediately. Repeat with the remaining 2 sandwiches.

Enjoy with Cakebread Cellars Pinot Noir or another medium-bodied red wine.

Pizza with Caramelized Onions, Belgian Endive, Gorgonzola, and Walnuts

MAKES FOUR 8-INCH PIZZAS

Belgian endive, toasted walnuts, and Gorgonzola make a satisfying winter salad—and a successful pizza topping. Brian first covers the pizza dough with a layer of caramelized onions, then sprinkles on the braised endive, crunchy nuts, and clumps of creamy Gorgonzola *dolce*, a young, mild version of the familiar Italian blue cheese. Cut the hot pie into thin wedges for an appetizer, or serve larger wedges with a salad for dinner.

2 large yellow onions, halved and thinly sliced

2 tablespoons extra-virgin olive oil

1 sprig fresh thyme

Kosher salt

3 Belgian endives

1 tablespoon unsalted butter

1/4 teaspoon sugar

1 teaspoon freshly squeezed lemon juice

1/2 cup balsamic vinegar

Pizza dough (page 192)

Cornmeal or durum flour for dusting

6 ounces Gorgonzola *dolce*

1/4 cup chopped toasted walnuts

1 tablespoon chopped flat-leaf parsley

Put the onions, olive oil, thyme sprig, and a large pinch of salt in a small saucepan over medium-low heat. Cover and cook, stirring occasionally, until the onions are soft, moist, and steaming in their own juices but not browned, about 30 minutes. Uncover, raise the heat to medium, and continue cooking, stirring often, until the onions are well caramelized and meltingly tender, 15 minutes or more depending on how moist they are.

Cut the endives crosswise into 1-inch pieces. Separate into individual layers. Discard the cores. Heat a skillet over medium heat. Add the butter, endive, sugar, lemon juice, and salt to taste. Cook until the endives are soft and tender, stirring occasionally to prevent browning, 5 to 10 minutes. You should have about 1 cup.

Bring the balsamic vinegar to a boil in a small saucepan. Simmer until reduced to 2 tablespoons, about 5 minutes. Let cool.

At least 45 minutes before baking, put a pizza stone on a rack in the bottom third of the oven and preheat the oven to its highest setting (500°F to 550°F).

With lightly floured fingers on a lightly floured work surface, flatten a ball of pizza dough into a round. Pick up the round with both hands and, grasping the round by an edge, rotate the dough clockwise between your fingertips, always holding it by the edge. As you rotate the dough, stretch it into an 8-inch circle; the dough will also stretch and lengthen from its own weight. Alternatively, drape the flattened round over your lightly floured knuckles and rotate the dough, moving your knuckles slightly farther apart, until the round stretches into an 8-inch circle.

Place the dough on a pizza peel lightly dusted with cornmeal or durum flour. Work quickly now to prevent sticking.

Spread one-quarter of the onion mixture over the dough. Scatter about 1/4 cup endive over the onions, then place several small spoonfuls of the cheese on top, using a total of $1^1/_2$ ounces. Slide onto the pizza stone and bake until the crust is brown and crisp, about 10 minutes. Remove from the oven. Scatter 1 tablespoon chopped walnuts and a sprinkle of parsley on top and drizzle with $1^1/_2$ teaspoons of the balsamic syrup. Cut into serving slices and serve while still warm. Repeat with the remaining 3 balls of dough.

Enjoy with Cakebread Cellars Dancing Bear Ranch Cabernet Sauvignon or another full-bodied red wine.

Blooms You Can Use

EVERY YEAR, JUST BEFORE Valentine's Day, a big bouquet arrives at the winery for Dolores. But it isn't fresh flowers. Tucked inside the florist wrap like long-stemmed roses is a bundle of red and white endive, the shapely heads still attached to their thick chicory roots.

With this whimsical gift, Richard Collins of California Vegetable Specialties thanks the good customers who have helped his endive business bloom, from 16,000 pounds the first year to more than 5 million pounds annually today. Rich almost single-handedly created this market. No one was growing endive commercially in the United States until he set out to do it as a young man just out of college. He researched the production method in Europe, then planted his first five acres in Vacaville, California, near Napa Valley.

Even many of the Workshop chefs have no idea how endive grows. The process starts with the planting of a type of chicory, which sends a thick taproot into the soil and sprouts coarse, bitter greens above ground. The greens are sold for livestock feed and the roots dug up. After a dormant season in cold storage, the roots are transferred to a controlled-atmosphere forcing room where they "bloom," sending up the tight, pale heads most people refer to as Belgian endive.

We often use California Vegetable Specialties endive as an edible spoon for stand-up hors d'oeuvres. Brian might fill the spears with beet tartare, crab salad, or blue cheese with port-soaked walnuts. Or he might slice and sauté the endive to use in a savory galette and on pizza (opposite page). Rich grows both red and white varieties, and they're always plump, pale, and blemish free. At the market, avoid endives that are "greening" from exposure to light; they may be bitter.

AM+ 3Y

PASTA AND RICE

QUALITE
CTB
CERTIFIEE
No 8

SPRING

SUMMER

FALL

WINTER

Penne with Pea Pesto, Sugar Snap Peas, and Pecorino

SERVES 6

From late spring to early summer, when our winery garden is producing tender peas, Brian makes a delicate pasta sauce with them. It's not worth making the pesto with starchy peas, so wait for that perfect cusp-of-summer moment. Serve this pasta as a first course, followed by Slow-Roasted King Salmon with Garden Herbs (page 110) or spring lamb chops. On another occasion, spread the pea pesto on crostini for an hors d'oeuvre.

PEA PESTO

3/4 cup shelled English peas (from about 3/4 pound fresh peas)

1 small clove garlic, smashed

1 teaspoon chopped fresh mint

2 tablespoons freshly grated pecorino cheese, plus more for topping

Kosher salt

1/4 cup extra-virgin olive oil

1 pound dried penne or other short pasta

2 tablespoons extra-virgin olive oil

1 cup shelled English peas (from about 1 pound fresh peas)

1/2 pound sugar snap peas, ends trimmed, halved crosswise

Freshly ground black pepper

For the pea pesto: Bring a small saucepan of water to a boil over high heat. Add the peas and blanch for 30 seconds, or a little longer if the peas are large. Drain and cool quickly in ice water, then drain again. Place the peas in a food processor with the garlic, mint, pecorino, and a pinch of salt. Pulse until well chopped. With the motor running, add the olive oil through the feed tube. Puree until the pesto is nearly but not completely smooth. A slightly coarse texture is pleasing.

Bring a large pot of salted water to a boil over high heat. Add the pasta and cook until al dente.

While the pasta cooks, warm the olive oil in a large pot over medium heat. Add the English peas and a pinch of salt. Sauté for about 2 minutes, then add 1/2 cup of the boiling pasta water. Simmer until the peas are almost tender, about 5 minutes, adding more hot pasta water if necessary. Add the sugar snap peas and sauté until they lose their raw taste, 1 to 2 minutes.

Set aside about 1 cup of the pasta water, then drain the pasta. Return it to the hot pot and add the braised peas, pea pesto, and several grinds of black pepper. Toss well, moistening with some of the reserved pasta water. Divide among 6 warm bowls. Top each portion with a little grated pecorino. Serve immediately.

Enjoy with Cakebread Cellars Napa Valley Chardonnay or another medium- to full-bodied white wine.

Whole-Wheat Linguine with Asparagus, Bacon, Garlic, and Parmesan

SERVES 6

When our wine-club members receive their wine shipment, we include a recipe that we enjoy with the featured bottle. Cakebread resident chef Tom Sixsmith devised this pasta preparation to accompany the Chardonnay Reserve, but you may find that you want to make the dish weekly in asparagus season. The nutty whole-wheat pasta and smoky bacon help combat the notion that asparagus doesn't go with wine.

1½ pounds large asparagus

6 slices bacon, preferably thick-cut

1 pound whole-wheat linguine

Kosher salt and freshly ground black pepper

3 cloves garlic, minced

3 tablespoons extra-virgin olive oil

¼ cup freshly grated Parmesan cheese, plus more for garnish

Snap off the woody ends of the asparagus. Slice the spears about ¼ inch thick on a sharp diagonal, so that the pieces are roughly 1½ inches long. Cut the bacon into ½-inch-wide pieces.

Bring a large pot of salted water to a boil over high heat. Add the pasta and cook until al dente.

While the pasta cooks, heat a large skillet over moderately high heat. Add the bacon and cook until it renders some of its fat and begins to crisp, about 4 minutes. Add the asparagus and sauté, stirring, until it softens slightly, about 3 minutes. Season with salt and pepper. Add the garlic and olive oil and cook for about 1 minute to release the garlic fragrance.

Set aside about 1 cup of the pasta water, then drain the pasta. Return it to the hot pot. Add the contents of the skillet and the grated cheese. Toss well, adding reserved pasta water as needed to moisten the pasta. Divide among 6 warm bowls. Top each portion with a little additional Parmesan. Serve immediately.

Enjoy with Cakebread Cellars Chardonnay Reserve or another rich, barrel-fermented Chardonnay.

Rigatoni with Eggplant, Italian Sausage, and Tomato

SERVES 8

When Jody Denton participated in the 2006 Workshop, he made delicate ricotta gnocchi in a sauce similar to the one outlined here. Chef Denton used wild boar sausage from Broken Arrow Ranch (see page 144), our longtime game supplier, but Italian pork sausage is a more readily available substitute. It takes practice to master gnocchi, but Chef Denton's delicious sauce is just as appealing with rigatoni.

1 small globe eggplant, about 1 pound, peeled, cut into 1-inch cubes

Kosher salt

4 tablespoons extra-virgin olive oil

3/4 pound sweet or hot Italian sausage, casing removed

2 cloves garlic, minced

3 cups peeled, seeded, and diced plum tomatoes (fresh or canned)

3-inch piece of Parmesan rind (optional)

1/4 cup torn fresh basil leaves

Freshly ground black pepper

1 pound rigatoni or penne

1/4 cup freshly grated Parmesan cheese, plus more for passing

Put the eggplant cubes in a colander set over a bowl. Add 2 teaspoons salt and toss well. Let drain for 30 minutes. Squeeze the eggplant cubes vigorously to release additional moisture, then set aside on paper towels.

In a large nonstick skillet, heat 2 tablespoons olive oil over medium-high heat. Add the eggplant and sauté until browned in spots and tender, about 10 minutes. (Taste to be sure.)

In a large pot, heat the remaining 2 tablespoons olive oil over medium heat. Add the sausage and cook, breaking it up with a wooden spoon, until it is finely crumbled and no longer pink, about 5 minutes. Add the garlic and sauté briefly to release its fragrance. Add the tomatoes, Parmesan rind, and basil. Bring to a simmer and cook for about 10 minutes to blend the flavors. Stir in the eggplant. Season with salt and pepper and simmer gently for about 5 minutes. Remove the Parmesan rind.

Bring a large pot of salted water to a boil over high heat. Add the pasta and cook until al dente. Set aside 1 cup of the pasta water, then drain the pasta and add it to the sauce. Toss well, add the cheese, and toss again, moistening with reserved pasta water if needed. Serve immediately in 8 warm bowls and pass additional Parmesan cheese.

Enjoy with Cakebread Cellars Zinfandel or another robust red wine.

Shellfish and Chorizo Paella

SERVES 6

Brian teaches a paella class at the winery occasionally to help take the fear out of preparing rice the Spanish way. It's a great dish for parties because guests love watching paella come together, the flavors and fragrance building as ingredients are added. Brian cooks his paella by the traditional method, outdoors over a hardwood fire. Gauging the heat of the fire is the only challenge; if it is too hot, the rice will scorch. Be sure to let the coals burn down until they are well covered with white ash before starting. And if you still lack confidence after trying this recipe, sign up for the class.

   Paella tastes best warm, not hot, so allow for some cooling time.

$1/2$ cup Cakebread Cellars Sauvignon Blanc or other dry white wine

1 tablespoon Spanish smoked sweet paprika (*pimentón de la Vera dulce*)

$1/4$ teaspoon saffron threads

18 large shell-on shrimp

$1/4$ cup plus 3 tablespoons extra-virgin olive oil

$3/4$ pound sea scallops

Kosher salt

2 large yellow onions, minced

1 large red bell pepper, minced

$1^1/2$ cups canned plum tomatoes, pureed

2 cups medium-grain Spanish rice, preferably Bomba or Calasparra variety

4 to 6 cups hot fish stock (page 191)

$1^1/2$ cups cooked chickpeas

1 pound manila or cherrystone clams

$3/4$ pound mussels

2 ounces Spanish chorizo, thinly sliced on the diagonal

$1/2$ cup thinly sliced scallions (green part only)

In a small saucepan, combine the wine, paprika, and saffron. Bring to a boil over high heat, then cover and set aside to steep for 30 minutes.

   With a serrated knife, slit the shrimp down the back and lift out the black vein but leave the shell on.

   Prepare a medium-hot charcoal fire. When the coals are well coated with white ash, put a 15-inch paella pan on the grill rack to preheat. Add $1/4$ cup olive oil. When the oil is hot, add the shrimp and cook until pink on both sides, about $1^1/2$ minutes per side, then set the shrimp aside. They will not be fully cooked.

   Season the scallops with salt. Add another tablespoon of olive oil to the pan and sear the scallops until lightly browned on both sides, about 1 minute per side. Set them aside. They will not be fully cooked.

   Add the remaining 2 tablespoons olive oil to the pan. Add the onions, bell pepper, and a pinch of salt. Cook, stirring, until the onions and pepper are soft and sweet, about 10 minutes. Add the tomato puree and cook, stirring, for about 5 minutes to develop flavor. Add the rice and cook, stirring, until hot to the touch, 1 to 2 minutes.

   Add 4 cups hot stock, the chickpeas, and the wine mixture. Stir to blend, then season to taste with salt. Cook at a steady simmer without stirring until the rice is about half done, 10 to 12 minutes, then add the clams, pushing them down into the soupy rice. Place the mussels evenly around the pan, setting them slender end up in the rice. Distribute the scallops evenly, tucking them into the rice. When the rice has cooked about 5 minutes more, add the shrimp, then the chorizo, distributing them evenly. Scatter the scallions over all. Add more hot stock only if the rice looks dry. Try not to stir, but if you fear that the rice may be scorching on the bottom, stir briefly to redistribute it.

Continue cooking until the rice is barely al dente, about 20 minutes; it will finish cooking off the heat. Drape the pan loosely with a kitchen towel and let the paella rest at room temperature for at least 15 minutes before serving.

Enjoy with Cakebread Cellars Chardonnay or another full-bodied white wine.

Plate Art

DOLORES HAS INVITED the Napa Valley College Potters Guild to participate in the Workshop for many years, in the belief that supporting local arts helps strengthen the community. The artists who belong to the guild show their wares at the Workshop's opening-day farmers' market and chat with the chefs about their ceramic techniques.

The winery has purchased quite a lot of this striking pottery over the years. (Many of the recipes in this book were photographed on Potters Guild pieces; see pages 43, 63, 87, 95, and 151.) We use the platters for passed hors d'oeuvres when we entertain, and we bring out many

pieces for chefs to use during the Workshop. They are always excited to present their food on these hand-crafted dishes, a marriage that highlights the artistry of both.

On occasion, we have taken the Workshop chefs to visit the potting studio at Napa Valley College, where instructor Rhue Bruggeman encourages them to try their hand at the potter's wheel. That's when the chefs realize that, as effortless as it seems when the artist does it, throwing clay takes great focus and skill. Most of them feel as awkward at the potter's wheel as non-cooks do when they pick up a chef's knife.

Mexican-Style Green Rice (*Arroz Verde*)

SERVES 6

When your menu calls for rice pilaf, consider this aromatic *arroz verde* instead. The flavor is more herbaceous than spicy, with a subtle sweetness from sautéed onion. You don't have to limit the rice to occasions when you are serving Mexican food. Try it with grilled pork tenderloin, skirt steaks, or a pork stew.

1 large poblano chile

1 large jalapeño chile

2 1/2 cups chicken stock (page 190) or vegetable stock (page 191)

1/4 cup cilantro leaves, firmly packed

2 tablespoons vegetable oil

1 large white onion, minced

1 1/2 cups long-grain white rice

Kosher salt

Under a preheated broiler or directly over a gas flame, roast the poblano and jalapeño chiles until blackened and blistered on all sides. Let cool, then peel, seed, and chop coarsely. Put 1 cup of the stock in a blender with the cilantro and roasted chiles and puree until smooth.

Heat the oil in a medium saucepan over medium heat. Add the onion and sauté until slightly softened, about 5 minutes. Add the rice and cook, stirring, for about 1 minute to toast the rice lightly. Add the remaining 1 1/2 cups stock and the chile puree. Bring to a boil, cover, reduce the heat to low, and cook for 18 minutes. Turn off the heat and let rest, covered, for 10 minutes. Fluff with a fork and season to taste with salt, then transfer to a serving bowl.

Pasta with Ned's Creamy Crab Sauce

SERVES 6 TO 8

In the minds of many West Coast chefs, the Dungeness crab is the ocean's finest crustacean. Canadian chef Ned Bell, who attended the 2004 Workshop, showcases the sweet meat in this pasta sauce, which gets some of its creamy body from pureed cauliflower. The dish is rich and worthy of the spotlight, so balance it with a simple butter lettuce salad in a tangy vinaigrette.

2 tablespoons unsalted butter

1/2 small yellow onion, diced

2 cloves garlic, minced

2 cups (about 1/2 medium head) chopped raw cauliflower

2 cups whole milk

1/4 teaspoon red chile flakes

Kosher salt

1/2 cup mascarpone

1 tablespoon Dijon mustard

1 pound short dried pasta, such as fusilli or penne

1 cup grated aged white Cheddar cheese

1/2 pound Dungeness crab meat

2 tablespoons thinly sliced fresh chives

Melt the butter in a medium saucepan over moderate heat. Add the onion and garlic and sauté until the onion softens slightly, about 5 minutes. Add the cauliflower, milk, chile flakes, and 1 teaspoon salt. Bring just to a simmer, then adjust the heat to simmer gently. Cook, uncovered, until the cauliflower is tender, 10 to 15 minutes. Puree in a blender. Transfer to a bowl and whisk in the mascarpone and mustard.

Bring a large pot of salted water to a boil over high heat. Add the pasta and boil until al dente. Drain and return the pasta to the warm pot. Add the cauliflower sauce and Cheddar and toss over moderately low heat until the cheese melts. Taste for salt. Add the crab meat and chives and toss again. Serve immediately in warm bowls.

Enjoy with Cakebread Cellars Napa Valley Chardonnay or another full-bodied white wine.

Dirty Rice with Fennel

SERVES 4

At the 1992 Workshop, Chef Jim Mills accompanied rabbit with New Orleans–style "dirty rice," a pilaf flavored with onion, celery, and chopped chicken livers. Brian makes the dish with Wehani rice, a nutty brown rice of basmati ancestry, created and grown exclusively by California's Lundberg Family Farms. Serve with Braised Chicken with Cipolline Onions and Carrots (opposite page; recipe on page 141) or a simple roast chicken, or as a main course with vegetable sides and a salad.

1 cup Lundberg Wehani rice or brown rice

Kosher salt

2 tablespoons unsalted butter

1/4 pound fresh chicken livers, trimmed

1/2 large fennel bulb, minced

1 celery rib, minced

3 scallions, white and green parts, minced

In a small saucepan, combine the rice and 2 cups water. Bring to a simmer over high heat, then cover, reduce the heat to low, and cook for 50 minutes. Season with 1/2 teaspoon salt, stirring it in with a fork. Re-cover and let the rice steam off the heat for 10 minutes.

Melt the butter in a large skillet over high heat. Season the livers with salt, then sear until browned on both sides, about 2 minutes. They should still be slightly soft to the touch. Set them aside. Add the fennel, celery, and scallions to the skillet and sauté until softened, 8 to 10 minutes. Dice the livers and add to the skillet. Cook, stirring, for about 1 minute, then add the rice and toss until blended. Serve immediately.

Barley Mushroom Risotto

SERVES 6

If you like risotto, you will love this creamy, heart-healthy variation made with barley. Pearled barley is not a whole grain, because it has had much of the bran removed, but it has a lot more fiber than white rice so it's a healthful choice. Chef David Koelling, a 1990 Workshop participant, adds mushrooms to his barley risotto to make the dish more substantial. Serve it in small portions as a first course or side dish—it would complement roast chicken—or in larger portions as a main course, with a salad.

1/4 ounce dried porcini

2 to 2 1/2 quarts chicken stock (page 190), simmering

3 tablespoons extra-virgin olive oil

1 medium yellow onion, chopped

1 large clove garlic, chopped

1 teaspoon chopped fresh thyme

1 1/2 cups pearl barley

1/2 cup dry white wine

1/3 pound fresh shiitake mushrooms, stems removed, cut into 1/2-inch dice

1/4 cup freshly grated Parmesan cheese

Kosher salt and freshly ground black pepper

Put the dried porcini in a small bowl and add 1/2 cup hot water. Let stand for 30 minutes. Lift the porcini out of their soaking liquid to leave any grit behind. Strain the liquid through a double thickness of dampened cheesecloth and add it to the stock. Chop the porcini.

In a large pot, warm the olive oil over medium heat. Add the onion, garlic, and thyme and cook until the onion is translucent, about 5 minutes. Add the barley and cook, stirring, until it is hot throughout, 1 to 2 minutes.

Add the wine and simmer until it has almost evaporated. Begin adding the simmering stock, 1 cup at a time, stirring frequently and adding more stock only when the previous addition has been absorbed.

After 10 minutes, add the shiitake and chopped porcini. Continue cooking until the barley is al dente, or pleasantly firm but not chewy, about 35 minutes longer. Stir in the cheese, season with salt and pepper, and serve immediately.

Enjoy with Cakebread Cellars Chardonnay Reserve or Pinot Noir.

Pappardelle with Duck Bolognese and Tuscan Kale

SERVES 6

The Liberty Ducks we get from Sonoma County Poultry (see page 147) are fed an all-natural diet and allowed to mature for several more weeks than most commercial ducks. As a result, they develop more flavor. The meaty duck legs, braised slowly with aromatic vegetables, make a robust pasta sauce similar in richness and depth to a classic *bolognese*. Brian shreds the tender duck meat after it's braised and adds chopped Tuscan kale to the sauce to introduce some fresh garden flavor.

4 duck legs (about 2 pounds)

Kosher salt and freshly ground black pepper

2 tablespoons extra-virgin olive oil

1/2 cup (2 to 3 ounces) finely diced pancetta

2 medium yellow onions, finely minced

2 celery ribs, finely minced

1 carrot, finely minced

2 tablespoons chopped flat-leaf parsley

1 1/2 cups canned plum tomatoes, broken up by hand

1/2 cup Cakebread Cellars Sauvignon Blanc or other dry white wine

1 1/2 cups chicken stock (page 190)

Parmesan rind (optional)

1 bunch (10 to 12 ounces) Tuscan kale, central rib removed

1/4 cup whole milk

1 pound fresh *pappardelle*, dried *mafaldine*, or other long, wide ribbon pasta

Freshly grated Parmesan cheese (optional)

Trim the excess flap of skin on each duck leg and remove visible fat. Season all over with salt and pepper. Heat the olive oil in a large pot over high heat. Add the duck, skin side down, and brown on all sides, about 5 minutes. Transfer the duck to a platter. Pour off all but 2 tablespoons fat.

Add the pancetta to the pot and cook over medium heat until it renders some of its fat and begins to crisp. Add the onions, celery, carrot, and parsley and sauté until the vegetables are softened, about 10 minutes. Add the tomatoes and wine. Bring to a simmer and reduce until slightly thickened, about 5 minutes. Return the duck to the pot, skin side up. Add the stock and the Parmesan rind (if using) and bring to a simmer. Cover and adjust the heat to maintain a gentle simmer. Simmer until the meat is tender and pulls readily from the bone, about 1 1/2 hours. Lift the duck legs out of the sauce and set them aside to cool.

Tear each kale leaf into 3 or 4 pieces. Bring a large pot of salted water to a boil over high heat. Add the kale and blanch for 30 seconds, then drain in a sieve and cool quickly under cold running water. Squeeze well to remove excess water. Finely chop.

Pull the duck meat off the bones and dice it. Return it to the sauce and reheat gently. Stir in the kale and the milk. Simmer gently for about 10 minutes to blend the flavors.

Bring a large pot of salted water to a boil over high heat. Add the pasta and cook until al dente. Set aside 1 cup of the pasta water, then drain the pasta and add it to the sauce. Toss well, moistening if necessary with some of the reserved pasta water. Divide among warm bowls and serve immediately. Pass Parmesan cheese, if desired.

Enjoy with Cakebread Cellars Carneros Pinot Noir or another rich Pinot Noir.

FISH AND SHELLFISH

SPRING

SUMMER

FALL

WINTER

Pan-Seared Catfish with Toasted Pecans and Carrot Emulsion

SERVES 6

When he attended the 1997 Workshop, Florida chef Pascal Oudin coated California salmon with a pecan crust, seared it, and paired it with a carrot emulsion. Brian has adapted the recipe to catfish, to give the dish some Floridian style, and replaced the crust with a toasted pecan garnish to make less work for home cooks. Serve with sautéed spinach or other wilted greens. On another occasion, prepare the silky carrot emulsion for grilled halibut or sea bass.

CARROT EMULSION

1/2 cup plus 1 tablespoon extra-virgin olive oil

1/3 cup minced shallots

2 teaspoons finely minced fresh ginger

1 teaspoon curry powder

3/4 cup dry sherry

2 cups fresh carrot juice

Kosher salt

2 tablespoons unsalted butter

1 teaspoon finely minced fresh ginger

1/2 cup coarsely chopped toasted pecans

6 (5-ounce) catfish fillets, about 1 inch thick

Freshly ground white pepper

4 tablespoons extra-virgin olive oil

For the carrot emulsion: In a medium saucepan, heat 1 tablespoon of the olive oil over moderate heat. Add the shallots, ginger, and curry powder. Sauté until the shallots are softened but not colored, about 5 minutes. Add the sherry, bring to a simmer, and reduce until almost dry. Add the carrot juice and simmer briskly until reduced to 3/4 cup, about 15 minutes. Strain through a fine sieve, pressing on the solids with a wooden spoon to extract all their flavor. Slowly whisk in the remaining 1/2 cup olive oil. Season with salt. Keep warm.

Melt the butter in a small skillet. Add the ginger and sauté for about 1 minute to release its fragrance. Add the pecans and toss to coat. Season with salt and keep warm.

Season the fish all over with salt and pepper. Set 2 nonstick skillets over medium-high heat and add 2 tablespoons olive oil to each. When the oil is almost smoking, put the fish in the skillets, flesh side down. Sear until browned, about 3 minutes, then turn and cook on the second side until it has browned and the catfish just flakes when probed with a fork, about 5 minutes longer, lowering the heat as needed to prevent burning.

To serve, spoon about 2 tablespoons of sauce onto each of 6 warm dinner plates. Top with a catfish fillet. Spoon some of the buttered pecans over the fish. Serve immediately.

Enjoy with Cakebread Cellars Napa Valley Chardonnay or another full-bodied white wine.

Slow-Roasted King Salmon with Garden Herbs

SERVES 8

Although we grill a lot of salmon at Cakebread Cellars, we have also come to love the creamy texture of salmon roasted slowly in a low oven. This gentle cooking method seems to accentuate salmon's richness and to yield a notably buttery result. Fish on the grill can overcook quickly, but the oven technique is much more forgiving. Accompany with Braised Radishes and Sugar Snap Peas (page 154).

One side (about 3¹/₂ pounds) wild king salmon, skin on

2 tablespoons extra-virgin olive oil

Kosher salt and freshly ground white pepper

1¹/₂ tablespoons chopped flat-leaf parsley

1 tablespoon thinly sliced fresh chives

1 teaspoon chopped fresh tarragon

Fleur de sel or other coarse sea salt

Lemon half

Preheat the oven to 275°F. With needle-nose pliers or tweezers, remove the salmon's fine pinbones. (You can feel these by running your fingers over the thickest part of the flesh in the head-to-tail direction.) Brush a baking sheet with 1 tablespoon of the olive oil, then put the fish on the baking sheet, skin side down, and rub the flesh with the remaining 1 tablespoon olive oil. Season with salt and pepper.

In a small bowl, combine the parsley, chives, and tarragon.

Bake the fish in the middle of the oven until white albumen, resembling cooked egg white, coagulates around the edges and on the surface, about 40 minutes. The fish should just barely flake when you press it, and you should be able to slide an offset spatula easily between the flesh and the skin. Using 2 spatulas, carefully transfer the whole fish to a platter. Scatter the herbs over the surface. Sprinkle with fleur de sel and squeeze the lemon half over the flesh. To serve, use an offset spatula to lift portions of fish off the skin.

Enjoy with Cakebread Cellars Napa Valley Chardonnay or another dry white wine with a lush texture.

Seared Sea Scallops with Chardonnay Creamed Corn

SERVES 4

Chef George Brown created this height-of-summer dish at the 2006 Workshop. He prepared the scallops in our wood-burning oven, but searing them in a hot skillet works as well. The creamed corn is thickened only by the corn's natural starch, released when the kernels are grated. The chef's idea of adding Chardonnay is a good one, as it helps to balance the corn's sweetness.

4 ears fresh corn, shucked

1 jalapeño chile

2 tablespoons unsalted butter

2 large shallots, minced

1/2 cup Cakebread Cellars Chardonnay

1/2 cup heavy cream

Kosher salt

Freshly squeezed lime juice

1 pound sea scallops

Freshly ground white pepper

1 tablespoon vegetable oil

With a large knife, slice the kernels from two of the corn cobs. In a separate bowl, using the coarse holes of a box grater, grate the kernels from the remaining two cobs.

Char the jalapeño over a gas flame or under a broiler until it is blackened all over. Let cool, then peel, seed, and mince.

Melt the butter in a medium saucepan over medium heat. Add the shallots and sliced corn kernels and sauté until the corn is tender, about 8 minutes. Add the wine and simmer until it has almost completely evaporated, 3 to 4 minutes. Add the cream, grated corn, minced jalapeño, and a pinch of salt. Simmer until the mixture thickens, about 3 minutes. Add lime juice to taste and keep warm over low heat.

Pull off the muscle on the side of each scallop. Season the scallops with salt and white pepper. Heat a large nonstick skillet over high heat. Add the vegetable oil. When the oil is almost smoking, add the scallops and sear until browned on the bottom, about 1 1/2 minutes. Turn and sear on the second side, about 1 1/2 minutes more.

Divide the creamed corn among 4 plates. Arrange the scallops on top of the creamed corn, dividing them evenly. Serve immediately.

Enjoy with Cakebread Cellars Napa Valley Chardonnay or another full-bodied white wine.

Grilled Mahimahi with Preserved Lemon Butter

SERVES 6

After a few weeks in a brine of salt and lemon juice, lemons develop an appetizing, lightly pickled taste. Brian makes Moroccan-style preserved lemons at the winery and keeps a stash on hand to use in recipes like this one. The seasoned butter would complement swordfish, sole, shrimp, or salmon, or you could dollop it on steamed mussels or clams. For this dish, Brian slathers the butter on the grilled fish served over Frank Stitt's Field Pea and Corn Salad (page 64), but wilted spinach would be an appealing accompaniment, too.

PRESERVED LEMON BUTTER

1/2 cup unsalted butter, softened

2 teaspoons minced rind of preserved lemons (page 192), pulp discarded

1 tablespoon minced scallion greens

1 teaspoon freshly squeezed lemon juice

Pinch of kosher salt

6 (5-ounce) skinless mahimahi fillets

Freshly ground white pepper

3 tablespoons extra-virgin olive oil

Field Pea and Corn Salad (page 64)

For the preserved lemon butter: Combine all the ingredients in a small bowl and mix with the back of a spoon until smooth.

Prepare a hot charcoal fire or preheat a gas grill to high. Season the fish on both sides with salt and white pepper. Brush on both sides with the olive oil and place on the grill, skinned side up. Cook for about 2 minutes, then rotate the fillets 90 degrees with tongs and cook for 2 minutes longer. Turn the fish skinned side down and cook for 2 minutes, then rotate 90 degrees and cook until the fish just flakes, about 2 minutes longer.

To serve, divide the salad among 6 dinner plates. Top with the fish. Immediately slather some of the preserved lemon butter on the hot fish, dividing it evenly. The butter will melt on contact. Serve immediately.

Enjoy with Cakebread Cellars Napa Valley Chardonnay or another full-bodied, silky white wine.

Seared Wild King Salmon with Cucumber, Red Onion, and Saffron Broth

SERVES 4

From chef Greg Higgins, a 2000 Workshop participant, comes this idea of pairing salmon with cucumbers, saffron, tarragon, and a creamy white-wine reduction. No surprise that a chef from the Pacific Northwest would know what flavors are sublime with salmon.

1/2 English (hothouse) cucumber, peeled, halved lengthwise, and seeded

1/2 red onion, thinly sliced

2 tablespoons unsalted butter

2 shallots, minced

1/2 cup Cakebread Cellars Sauvignon Blanc

Pinch of saffron threads

2 cups vegetable stock (page 191)

1/4 cup crème fraîche

2 teaspoons thinly sliced fresh chives, plus more for garnish

1/2 teaspoon minced fresh tarragon

Kosher salt

4 skinless salmon fillets (4 to 5 ounces each)

Freshly ground white pepper

2 tablespoons extra-virgin olive oil

Slice the cucumber halves on the diagonal about 1/3 inch thick. Bring a medium pot of salted water to a boil over high heat. Add the cucumbers and blanch for 20 seconds, then transfer with a wire-mesh skimmer to ice water to chill. Add the onion to the boiling water and blanch for 15 seconds. Drain and transfer to the ice water. When cool, drain and pat dry with paper towels.

In a saucepan, melt the butter over medium heat. Add the shallots and sauté until softened, about 8 minutes. Add the wine and saffron and simmer until almost dry. Add the stock and simmer until reduced by half. Whisk in the crème fraîche. Simmer until the sauce is reduced to about 1 cup. Strain through a fine-mesh sieve into a clean saucepan. Whisk in the chives and tarragon. Add the cucumbers and onions. Season with salt and keep warm over low heat while you cook the salmon.

With needle-nose pliers or tweezers, remove the salmon's fine pinbones. (You can feel these by running your fingers over the thickest part of the flesh.) Season the fish on both sides with salt and white pepper. Heat a large nonstick skillet over high heat. Add the olive oil. When the oil is hot, add the salmon, skinned side up. Sear until nicely browned, about 2 minutes, then turn and cook until the fish just flakes, about 3 minutes longer, lowering the heat as needed to prevent burning.

Divide the cucumbers, onions, and saffron broth evenly among 4 soup bowls. Top each serving with a salmon fillet. Garnish the salmon with a sprinkle of fresh chives. Serve immediately.

Enjoy with Cakebread Cellars Chardonnay or another medium-bodied white wine.

Pan-Seared Sturgeon with Thai Red Curry

SERVES 4

One of the benefits of working with so many chefs at the Workshop is that the experience sometimes takes us out of our comfort zone. We tend to shy away from spicy foods at the winery, but with this dish, Honolulu chef Alan Wong, who participated in the 1990 Workshop, reminded us that we don't need to be so cautious. Our wine can happily accompany a dish with Thai flavors if the heat is balanced with a touch of sweetness and citrus and mellowed with coconut milk. We were pleased—and admittedly surprised—at how seamlessly our Anderson Valley Pinot Noir married with Alan's red-curry sturgeon. Accompany the fish with stir-fried bok choy or spinach and steamed rice to soak up the luscious sauce.

4 tablespoons vegetable oil

1/2 small yellow onion, minced

1 tablespoon minced fresh ginger

2 cloves garlic, minced

1 1/2 teaspoons Thai red curry paste

1 cup chicken stock (page 190)

3-inch piece of fresh lemongrass, halved lengthwise and smacked with the side of a chef's knife

1 kaffir lime leaf, thawed if frozen, torn in half

1 cup canned coconut milk (shake can well before opening)

1 teaspoon Asian fish sauce

1/2 teaspoon sugar

4 (5-ounce) skinless sturgeon or halibut fillets

Kosher salt

Freshly ground white pepper

1/2 cup peeled, seeded, and diced tomato

2 tablespoons minced Thai basil

Heat 2 tablespoons of the oil in a 3-quart saucepan over moderate heat. Add the onion, ginger, and garlic and sauté for about 5 minutes to soften the onion. Add the curry paste and break it up with the back of a wooden spoon. Cook, stirring, for about 2 minutes to incorporate the paste. Stir in the chicken stock, lemongrass, and lime leaf. Simmer until the stock is reduced by half. Add the coconut milk, fish sauce, and sugar. Whisk to blend, then simmer gently until the mixture has reduced to a sauce consistency, about 2 minutes. Pass the sauce through a fine sieve into a small saucepan. You should have about 1 cup.

Season the fish on both sides with salt and white pepper. Put the remaining 2 tablespoons vegetable oil in a large nonstick skillet and set over high heat. When the oil is hot, add the fish, skinned side up. Sear until nicely browned, about 5 minutes, then turn and cook until the fish just flakes, about 3 minutes longer.

While the fish cooks, gently reheat the sauce. Just before serving, stir in the tomato and basil.

To serve, divide the sauce among 4 dinner plates. Top with the sturgeon. Serve immediately.

Enjoy with Cakebread Cellars Anderson Valley Pinot Noir or another full-bodied, concentrated Pinot Noir.

Roast Halibut with Chorizo and Spicy Tomato Broth

SERVES 4

Seasoned with chorizo, dried oregano, and cilantro, this deconstructed fish stew tastes like the specialty of some upscale restaurant in Mexico City. But it came to Cakebread Cellars from one of Denver's foremost chefs, Kevin Taylor, a 1997 Workshop participant. For a dinner party, you can make the tomato broth a couple of hours ahead, stopping after you add the cooked chorizo and potatoes. Then all you need to do at dinner time is steam the fish on this flavorful base. You could add some clams or shrimp to the pot as well.

1 tablespoon extra-virgin olive oil

2 (5- to 6-ounce) whole Mexican-style chorizo sausages

1 pound fingerling potatoes

TOMATO BROTH

2 tablespoons extra-virgin olive oil

1/2 large red bell pepper, cut into 1/4-inch dice

1/2 large yellow bell pepper, cut into 1/4-inch dice

3 large cloves garlic, minced

1/4 teaspoon red chile flakes

2 cups peeled, seeded, and diced fresh tomatoes, or 2 cups canned whole peeled tomatoes in puree, broken up by hand

1/2 teaspoon dried Mexican oregano

2 cups chicken stock (page 190) or vegetable stock (page 191)

1/2 cup Cakebread Cellars Sauvignon Blanc

Kosher salt

4 (4- to 5-ounce) skinless halibut or cod fillets

Freshly ground black pepper

1 to 2 tablespoons chopped cilantro for garnish

Preheat the oven to 400°F. Heat the olive oil in a small ovenproof skillet over moderate heat. Add the chorizo and brown on all sides, about 3 minutes. Transfer the skillet to the oven and roast until the sausages feel firm, about 5 minutes. Set aside to cool slightly, then cut into 1-inch-thick slices.

Put the potatoes in a saucepan with salted water to cover by 1 inch. Bring to a boil, adjust the heat to maintain a simmer, and cook until the potatoes are tender when pierced, about 15 minutes. Drain and let cool. Peel, then cut into 1-inch chunks.

For the tomato broth: Heat the olive oil in a large pot over high heat. Add the bell peppers and sauté, stirring, for about 3 minutes to soften them, then add the garlic and chile flakes. Lower the heat and cook for about 1 minute to release the garlic fragrance, then add the tomatoes and the oregano, rubbing the herb between your fingers. Simmer briskly until the tomatoes soften, about 2 minutes, then add the stock and wine. Simmer for about 5 minutes to thicken the liquid slightly, then add the chorizo and potatoes. Simmer for 5 minutes to develop the flavor. Taste and adjust the seasoning.

Season the fish on both sides with salt and pepper. Arrange the fillets on top of the stew, then cover and simmer gently until the fish is fully cooked, about 10 minutes. Divide the chorizo, potatoes, and broth among 4 soup bowls, then top each portion with a fish fillet. Garnish with chopped cilantro. Serve immediately.

Enjoy with Cakebread Cellars Carneros Pinot Noir or another medium-bodied red wine with zesty fruit.

Black Cod with Clams, Chanterelles, and *Fregola*

SERVES 4

Also known as sablefish, black cod thrives in the cold waters off the Pacific Coast, from California to Alaska. The fishery is managed sustainably, so many chefs have turned to black cod as a replacement for the more threatened Chilean sea bass. If you have ever had smoked sablefish in a New York delicatessen, you have eaten black cod. It is an oily fish, rich in heart-healthy omega-3 fatty acids. Chef Bruce Hill, who attended the 1998 Workshop, makes it the centerpiece of this inspired East-West seafood stew, which relies on *fregola*—a toasty, couscous-like Sardinian pasta—for texture and Japanese miso for flavor depth. *Dashi* is Japanese stock.

MUSHROOM *DASHI*

3 dried shiitake mushroom caps

1 cup warm water

2 tablespoons soy sauce

2 tablespoons mirin (sweet Japanese rice wine)

3/4 cup *fregola* (Sardinian pasta; see Ingredient Resources, page 193)

3 tablespoons extra-virgin olive oil

1/2 large yellow onion, diced

1 medium fennel bulb, diced

1/4 pound fresh chanterelle mushrooms, trimmed, cut into roughly 1-inch chunks

Kosher salt and freshly ground black pepper

4 black cod (sablefish) fillets, skin on, about 4 ounces each

2 tablespoons vegetable oil

3 dozen (about 1 3/4 pounds) manila clams

1 tablespoon red miso

1 tablespoon coarsely chopped fresh cilantro

Freshly squeezed lemon juice (optional)

For the mushroom *dashi*: Put the shiitake and warm water in a small saucepan and let soften for 10 minutes. Add the soy sauce and mirin and bring to a boil over high heat. Remove from the heat and let steep for 20 minutes. Strain.

Bring a medium pot of salted water to a boil. Add the *fregola* and boil until al dente. Drain.

Heat the olive oil in a large skillet over high heat. Add the onion and fennel and sauté until softened and lightly caramelized, about 5 minutes. Add the chanterelles and season with salt and pepper. Sauté until they soften and color slightly, about 3 minutes. Keep warm.

Season the cod with salt and pepper. Heat a cast-iron skillet over moderately high heat. Add the 2 tablespoons vegetable oil. When the oil is hot, put the fish in the skillet, interior side down. Sear until lightly browned in spots, about 2 minutes, then turn and cook until the flesh turns white and begins to flake, about 4 minutes longer.

While the fish cooks, put the clams in a large pot and add the mushroom *dashi*. Bring to a boil over high heat, cover, and steam until the clams open, about 2 minutes. Discard any that fail to open.

Ladle about 1/4 cup of the clam juices into a small bowl, add the miso, and whisk to blend. Return these juices to the clam pot, then gently stir in the onions, fennel, mushrooms, *fregola*, and cilantro. Taste and add a bit of lemon juice if desired.

Divide the clams and vegetables among 4 warm bowls, making a space in the center for the fish. Place a cod fillet in the center of each bowl. Serve immediately.

Enjoy with Cakebread Cellars Napa Valley Chardonnay or a similarly full-bodied white wine with a silky texture.

Sand Dabs with Fresh Zante Currants

SERVES 2

This ten-minute recipe is California chef Ken Frank's riff on the French classic, sole Véronique. Chef Frank substitutes a Northern California delicacy—bone-in sand dabs—and the tiny and tasty dark grapes known as Zante currants. The fish are lightly floured and sautéed, then sauced with warmed grapes, melted butter, parsley, and lemon. You can use the same preparation on any delicate fish, such as petrale or Dover sole.

1 cup all-purpose flour

1 1/2 teaspoons kosher salt

Freshly ground black pepper

4 pan-ready sand dabs, about 3 ounces each

1/3 cup vegetable oil

4 tablespoons unsalted butter

1 large shallot, minced

1/4 cup stemmed fresh Zante currants (also known as Black Corinth grapes or champagne grapes)

1 heaping tablespoon chopped flat-leaf parsley

1/2 lemon

In a pie tin, combine the flour, salt, and several grinds of pepper. Mix to blend. Dredge the fish lightly in the seasoned flour.

Heat the vegetable oil and 1 tablespoon of the butter in a large skillet over medium-high heat. When the butter begins to brown and sizzle, add the fish and sauté on both sides until lightly browned, 2 to 2 1/2 minutes per side. Sand dabs are delicate and cook quickly.

Divide the fish between two warm dinner plates. Drain all the fat from the pan and wipe the pan clean with a paper towel. Off the heat, add the remaining 3 tablespoons butter. Return the pan to medium heat and add the shallot. Sauté until the shallot softens slightly, about 1 minute, then add the grapes and sauté for about 30 seconds to soften the grapes slightly. Do not let them collapse. Remove from the heat and stir in the parsley. Spoon the grapes and butter over the fish, dividing them evenly. Squeeze a little lemon juice over each portion and serve immediately.

Enjoy with Cakebread Cellars Sauvignon Blanc or another crisp white wine.

San Francisco Cioppino

SERVES 8

Who better to provide a cioppino recipe than Jesse Llapitan, the executive chef of San Francisco's Palace Hotel, the city's grande dame? Every San Franciscan puts his or her own stamp on this rustic fisherman's stew, but the Dungeness crab is nonnegotiable. Chef Llapitan attended the 2005 Workshop.

2 cooked Dungeness crabs (about 1¹/2 pounds each)

4 tablepoons extra-virgin olive oil, plus more for garnish

1 large yellow onion, minced

1 celery rib, minced

¹/2 fennel bulb, minced

2 cloves garlic, minced

¹/2 teaspoon red chile flakes

1 cup Cakebread Cellars Sauvignon Blanc

1 quart fish stock (page 191)

2 cups tomato puree (canned is okay)

2 bay leaves

6 fresh basil leaves, chopped

Kosher salt

2 dozen manila clams

2 dozen mussels

³/4 pound large shrimp, peeled and deveined

1 to 1¹/4 pounds skinless halibut, sea bass, or other firm white fish, cut into 1¹/2-inch cubes

2 tablespoons chopped flat-leaf parsley for garnish

For each crab, detach the crab legs from the body by hand. With a mallet, crack the legs and claws. Holding the crab from underneath, lift off and discard the hard top shell. Turn the crab over; lift off and discard the triangular tail flap and the feathery gills along both sides. Quarter the body and pick out the meat. Reserve the body shells for the fish stock if desired.

Heat a large, wide 8-quart pot over moderately low heat. Add the olive oil. When the oil is hot, add the onion, celery, fennel, garlic, and chile flakes. Sauté until the vegetables are soft and sweet, 10 to 15 minutes. Add the wine, raise the heat to high, and bring to a boil. Add the fish stock, tomato puree, bay leaves, basil, and salt to taste. Simmer gently until reduced to the texture of a thin tomato sauce, 15 to 20 minutes.

Add the clams and mussels. Cover and cook over high heat until the shellfish begin to open. Add the crab legs and the shrimp. Cover and simmer for about 2 minutes, then add the halibut and the shelled crab meat. To keep the halibut in large chunks, don't stir it into the cioppino; cover the pot and let the fish steam on the surface until white throughout, about 7 minutes. Serve immediately in large bowls, dividing the fish and shellfish evenly and ladling the broth around. Garnish with chopped parsley.

Enjoy with Cakebread Cellars Napa Valley Chardonnay or another medium- to full-bodied white wine.

MEAT AND POULTRY

SPRING

SUMMER

FALL

WINTER

Moroccan Lamb Brochettes with Cumin Salt

SERVES 4

The spring release of Rubaiyat, our red wine blend, is a festive occasion at the winery. We invite our wine-club members to come sample the new release, and we set up several food stations in our courtyard. If the weather cooperates, the day is as much fun for the culinary staff as it is for our guests. Brian devises dishes expressly for the featured wines—not just Rubaiyat but other current releases, too. These juicy lamb kebabs, scented with North African spices, were a hit one year with Cakebread Cellars Syrah. Accompany with Carrot, Fennel, and Green Olive Slaw (page 56).

1 pound ground lamb, preferably from the shoulder

1 yellow onion, coarsely grated

2 tablespoons chopped flat-leaf parsley

1 teaspoon chopped fresh mint

1 teaspoon *ras el hanout* (see Note)

1 teaspoon kosher salt

CUMIN SALT

1 tablespoon cumin seeds

2 tablespoons kosher salt

4 lemon wedges for serving

Put the lamb, onion, parsley, mint, *ras el hanout*, and salt in a bowl. Mix with your hands until blended. Fry a small amount of the mixture in a nonstick skillet to taste the seasoning. Adjust if necessary.

Divide the meat mixture into 8 equal portions, each weighing roughly 2 ounces. With lightly oiled hands, mold each portion around a 12-inch bamboo or metal skewer, forming a neat sausage shape about 6 inches long and squeezing the meat so it clings to the skewer. You can assemble the kebabs several hours ahead; cover and refrigerate.

For the cumin salt: Toast the cumin seeds in a dry skillet over medium heat, shaking the skillet constantly until the seeds are fragrant and beginning to smoke. Pound them fine in a mortar, then stir in the salt.

Prepare a hot charcoal fire or preheat a gas grill to high. Lightly oil the grill with a rag dipped in vegetable oil. If you are using bamboo skewers, prepare two doubled sheets of aluminum foil that you can position underneath the exposed ends of the skewers so they don't burn. Place the skewers on the grill so that the exposed ends rest over the foil. (If you are using metal skewers, you don't need to take this precaution.) Grill, turning as needed, until the lamb is firm to the touch, 6 to 7 minutes.

Serve 2 skewers per person, accompanying each portion with a lemon wedge and a small ramekin of cumin salt.

NOTE: *Ras el hanout* is a Moroccan spice blend available from well-stocked spice merchants such as Whole Spice (see page 126).

Enjoy with Cakebread Cellars Carneros Syrah or another substantial red wine.

Spice Valley

UNTIL SHULI MADMONE entered our lives, we relied on the bountiful fresh-cut herbs in the winery garden and on a conventional spice pantry for seasoning.

But in 2008, when Shuli and his wife, Ronit, opened Whole Spice, their tantalizing shop in Napa's Oxbow Public Market, Brian became one of their most avid customers and students. The shop's vast collection of spices and seasonings in big glass jars was as alluring to him as candy is to a kid, and his discoveries began to infiltrate winery menus. He seasoned ground lamb kebabs with Moroccan *ras el hanout*; rubbed *za'atar* on roast chicken and Indian coriander on fresh tuna; and substituted the more fragrant Aleppo pepper from Syria and espelette pepper from France for cayenne. Shuli's seasoned salts, such as truffle salt and hibiscus salt, expanded our flavor world, too.

Brian invited Shuli to participate in the Workshop and help introduce participants to a broader range of seasonings. Whole Spice always provides a selection of unusual spices and spice blends, like *zhug,* a fiery mixture from Yemen used to finish dishes. In tastings at the winery, we have found that warm spices, used judiciously in our cooking, can bring out aromatic components in the accompanying wine. Brian's Indian Lentil Soup (page 71) highlights the toastiness of our barrel-fermented Chardonnay, a reminder that many possible wine and food affinities remain unexplored.

Braised Pork Ribs with Blood Orange, Fennel, and Black Olives

SERVES 6

Country-style ribs, from the shoulder end of the pork loin, turn succulent with long, slow braising. In late winter and early spring, when California's blood orange harvest is peaking, Brian adds their tangy juice to the braise, along with fennel wedges and kalamata olives. Like many braises, this dish reheats well. Serve with wide ribbon noodles, such as *pappardelle*.

3 pounds bone-in country-style pork ribs or shoulder chops

Kosher salt and freshly ground black pepper

4 tablespoons olive oil

3 medium fennel bulbs, cut into thick wedges

3 cloves garlic, thinly sliced

1 cup peeled and chopped plum tomatoes, fresh or canned

1/2 cup freshly squeezed blood orange juice

1 teaspoon honey

1 cup pitted kalamata olives

1 bay leaf

1 wide strip of blood orange zest

2 tablespoons chopped fennel fronds for garnish

Season the pork all over with salt and pepper. Heat a large, wide pot over high heat, then add the olive oil. When the oil is hot, add the pork and brown on all sides, about 5 minutes. Transfer the pork to a platter. Add the fennel wedges to the same pot and sear until lightly browned on both cut sides, about 2 minutes. Set the fennel aside.

Return the pot to low heat and add the garlic. Sauté for about 1 minute, stirring to release its fragrance, then add the tomatoes, orange juice, and honey. Stir with a wooden spoon to release any browned bits on the bottom of the pot. Return the pork to the pot, then add the olives, bay leaf, and orange zest. Bring to a boil, then cover, reduce the heat to maintain a gentle simmer, and cook until the pork is fork-tender, about 1 1/2 hours, turning it over in the sauce halfway through.

Transfer the pork to a platter with tongs and keep warm. Discard the bay leaf and orange zest. Add the fennel wedges to the pot. If necessary, add a little water so that the liquid comes about halfway up the sides of the fennel. Cover and cook until the fennel is tender, about 15 minutes. Return the pork to the pot and reheat, turning to coat it with the sauce. Divide the pork and fennel among 6 plates and spoon the sauce over them. Garnish with the chopped fennel fronds and serve immediately.

Enjoy with Cakebread Cellars Benchlands Select Cabernet Sauvignon or another red wine with firm structure and concentration.

Chicken *Mole Verde*

SERVES 6

Brian mastered *mole verde* under the tutelage of Brenda Godinez, a Cakebread staffer who creates exquisite flower arrangements for the winery. Brenda taught Brian that a proper mole requires many steps: almost every ingredient needs to be fried or toasted first to deepen its flavor. The *mole verde*, or green mole, relies on fresh chiles, tomatillos, and cilantro for its emerald color. When well made, the mole is velvety smooth. This recipe features chicken, but we sometimes use duck legs or pork. Truly, the spotlight is on the sauce. Serve with rice and a salad.

Note that this recipe makes twice as much mole (the sauce, not the chicken) as you need to serve six people. But why make mole in small amounts? It freezes well, giving you a running start on the next dinner.

CHICKEN

3 bone-in chicken breasts and 3 leg-thigh quarters

1 white onion, thickly sliced

2 cloves garlic, smashed

2 tablespoons kosher salt

MOLE

$1/4$ cup sesame seeds

3 tablespoons hulled pumpkin seeds

$1/4$ cup vegetable oil, plus more as needed

3 tablespoons raw peanuts

Pinch of ground ginger

Pinch of ground allspice

Pinch of ground cloves

$1/2$ ripe plantain (from a plantain cut crosswise), peeled and halved lengthwise (see Note)

2 whole serrano chiles, stemmed

1 large poblano chile, quartered and seeded

$1/2$ white onion, sliced

2 cloves garlic, peeled

2 pounds tomatillos, husked

1 corn tortilla

$1/2$ small head butter lettuce, or 1 romaine heart, coarsely chopped

For the chicken: Put the chicken parts in a large pot and add enough water to cover the meat by 2 inches. Add the onion, garlic, and salt. Bring to a simmer over high heat, skimming off any foam, then reduce the heat to maintain a gentle simmer. Cook until the meat begins to pull away from the drumstick and the thigh joint feels loose, about 30 minutes. Let cool in the broth, then strain and reserve the broth and chicken separately.

For the mole: Toast the sesame seeds and pumpkin seeds together in a large skillet over medium heat, stirring until the sesame seeds are golden brown and the pumpkin seeds have started to darken and pop, 5 to 6 minutes. Transfer to a bowl. Add the $1/4$ cup oil to the skillet and return to medium heat. When the oil is hot, fry the peanuts until golden, about 1 minute. With a slotted spoon, transfer the peanuts to the bowl with the seeds, leaving the oil behind. Add the ginger, allspice, and cloves to the seed mixture.

In the same skillet, in the oil remaining, fry the plantain over medium heat until lightly browned, about 3 minutes, then set the plantain aside. Add the serrano and poblano chiles, the onion, and the whole garlic cloves and fry until the chiles blister all over and the onion and garlic char in spots, 3 to 4 minutes. Set aside. Add the tomatillos to the same skillet and cook, turning, until they char and blister in spots, about 5 minutes. Set them aside.

Toast the tortilla directly over a gas flame or under a broiler until it blackens in spots and becomes crisp, about 1 minute. Let cool, then tear into pieces.

Put the seed mixture in a blender and blend on high speed, adding enough of the chicken broth—about 1 cup—to make a paste that is as smooth as possible. Transfer to a small bowl.

1 cup roughly chopped cilantro, plus more for garnish

1 small or 1/2 large avocado, pitted and peeled

1 1/2 teaspoons sugar, or to taste

Working in batches, put the tomatillos, plantain, chiles, onion, garlic, tortilla pieces, chopped lettuce, 1 cup cilantro, and the avocado in the blender and puree until smooth. (Put the tomatillos in first to have enough liquid to engage the blender.) Transfer to a bowl.

Put any leftover frying oil in a large pot and add enough additional vegetable oil to make 2 tablespoons. Set over medium heat and add the seed paste. Cook, stirring, until the paste becomes fragrant, about 1 minute. Stir in the tomatillo puree and bring to a simmer. Add 5 cups of the reserved chicken broth and simmer gently, stirring occasionally, for 1 1/4 hours to develop flavor. Add the sugar and season with salt. Remove half the sauce (about 5 cups) and freeze for later use.

Cut each chicken breast in half crosswise. Cut the leg-thigh quarters in half at the joint. You should have 12 pieces. Place the chicken parts in the mole and simmer until hot throughout. Thin with more chicken broth if desired.

Divide the mole and chicken among 6 warm bowls or plates. Garnish with chopped cilantro.

NOTE: A ripe plantain has a golden or even black exterior; unripe plantains are greenish outside.

Enjoy with Cakebread Cellars Sauvignon Blanc or another crisp and herbaceous white wine.

Tarragon Chicken with Drop Biscuits

SERVES 6

Chef Danielle Custer, who attended the 1997 Workshop, devised this modified potpie to use left-over Thanksgiving turkey. She wanted to make a version of the freezer-case classic but without the traditional bottom crust or the peas. Brian has added a California touch: asparagus from the winery garden, transforming the modest all-American potpie into a dish suitable for guests. Tender drop biscuits scented with chives take the place of a pastry crust.

QUICK CHICKEN STOCK

1 whole fresh chicken, about 4 pounds

1 large carrot, thinly sliced

1 celery rib, thinly sliced

1 yellow onion, halved and thinly sliced

2 bay leaves

1/2 teaspoon mixed pickling spice

1/4 teaspoon whole black peppercorns

1/4 teaspoon fennel seeds

1 sprig fresh rosemary

1 1/2 teaspoons kosher salt

4 tablespoons unsalted butter

1 yellow onion, cut into small dice

One 6-inch piece of leek (white and pale green part only), cut into small dice

1 large carrot, cut into small dice

1 celery rib, cut into small dice

1/4 cup all-purpose flour

1/4 cup heavy cream

1/4 cup thinly sliced scallions, white and pale green parts only

2 teaspoons chopped fresh tarragon

1 1/2 cups asparagus, sliced on the diagonal about 1/2 inch long

DROP BISCUITS

1 cup all-purpose flour

1 1/2 teaspoons baking powder

1/2 teaspoon kosher salt

1/2 cup whole milk

2 tablespoons unsalted butter, melted

1 large egg

2 tablespoons minced fresh chives

For the quick chicken stock: Cut up the chicken to yield 2 drumsticks, 2 thighs, 2 breasts, 2 wings, and a back. Put the parts in a large pot with 2 quarts cold water. Bring to a simmer over high heat, skimming off any foam. Add the carrot, celery, onion, bay leaves, pickling spice, peppercorns, fennel seeds, rosemary, and salt and adjust the heat to maintain a gentle simmer. Cook for 30 minutes, then remove from the heat and let cool. With tongs, lift the chicken from the stock and strain the stock. Set aside 1 quart; refrigerate or freeze the remaining stock for another use. Remove the chicken meat from the bones, shred the meat by hand, and discard the skin.

Preheat the oven to 400°F. In a large pot, melt the butter over medium heat. Add the onion, leek, carrot, and celery. Sauté until the vegetables soften, about 5 minutes. Add the flour and stir until blended. Add the reserved 1 quart chicken stock and bring to a simmer, whisking. Simmer, whisking occasionally, for about 5 minutes to thicken the sauce slightly. Whisk in the cream. Stir in the shredded chicken, scallions, and tarragon. Taste and adjust the seasoning.

Bring a small pot of salted water to a boil over high heat. Add the asparagus and boil for about 30 seconds, just to remove the raw taste. Drain and transfer to ice water to chill quickly. Drain well and add to the chicken mixture. Transfer to an 8 by 12-inch baking dish, or a dish of comparable size.

For the drop biscuits: In a large bowl, whisk together the flour, baking powder, and salt. In a small bowl, whisk together the milk, butter, egg, and chives. Add the liquid ingredients to the dry ingredients and stir just to moisten evenly; do not overmix. Drop 6 mounds of biscuit dough onto the chicken mixture, spacing them evenly.

Bake until the biscuits are lightly browned and the chicken mixture is bubbling, 25 to 30 minutes. Let rest for 5 to 10 minutes before serving.

Enjoy with Cakebread Cellars Napa Valley Chardonnay or another medium- to full-bodied white wine.

Grilled Leg of Lamb with Chimichurri

SERVES 8

Eduardo Pria, a 2002 Workshop participant and Mexico City native, is probably the most passionate chef we have ever had at the Workshop. He was overjoyed to be at the winery and expressed it with frequent hugs for all, usually coupled with an enthusiastic "I love you, man!" The Argentinian chimichurri sauce that Eduardo made for Don Watson's lamb was as exhilarating as he is. Brian has used the sauce frequently over the years, adapting it along the way. Prepared quickly in a blender, it is a vivid emerald green and like pesto in texture, with a fresh, zingy taste. It complements almost any grilled red meat—from leg of lamb to hanger steaks, flatiron steaks, or pork chops. Add roasted fingerling potatoes and Blistered Cherry Tomatoes (page 157) for an ideal summer meal. We also like chimichurri with grilled summer vegetables, such as zucchini, eggplant, and peppers. You can make the sauce a few hours ahead, but plan to use it the same day. It loses zip with time. Note that the lamb needs to marinate for at least two hours.

1 boneless, butterflied leg of lamb (about 3 1/2 pounds)

4 cloves garlic

1 1/2 teaspoons kosher salt

3 tablespoons extra-virgin olive oil

Freshly ground black pepper

CHIMICHURRI

1 cup firmly packed flat-leaf parsley leaves

1 cup firmly packed cilantro leaves

2 cloves garlic, mashed with the side of a chef's knife

1 jalapeño chile, seeds and veins removed, roughly chopped

1 teaspoon kosher salt

3/4 cup extra-virgin olive oil

1 tablespoon freshly squeezed lime juice

Trim external fat from the lamb, or ask the butcher to do so. Mince the garlic to a paste with the salt. Mix the garlic paste with the olive oil and several grinds of black pepper. Put the lamb in a shallow dish and rub all over with the garlic mixture. Cover with plastic wrap and refrigerate for at least 2 hours or, preferably, overnight.

For the chimichurri: In a blender, combine the parsley, cilantro, garlic, jalapeño, and salt. With the motor running, add the olive oil gradually, stopping once or twice to scrape down the sides of the jar. Blend until smooth. Transfer to a small bowl and stir in the lime juice. Taste and adjust the seasoning. Set aside at room temperature for 1 hour to develop flavor.

Prepare a hot charcoal fire or preheat a gas grill to high. Bring the lamb to room temperature. Grill the meat directly over the coals or flame, turning once with tongs, until an instant-read thermometer inserted in the thickest part of the muscle reaches 125°F (for medium-rare), 10 to 15 minutes per side. The muscles on a butterflied leg of lamb are not evenly thick; to prevent overcooking, test the thinner section first and remove that section when it is done by cutting between the muscles. Let the meat rest for at least 15 minutes before slicing to allow the juices to settle. Carve across the grain into thin slices and serve with chimichurri.

Enjoy with Cakebread Cellars Cabernet Sauvignon or another red wine with firm tannic structure.

Narsai's Assyrian Lamb with Pomegranate Marinade

SERVES 4

Narsai David's lamb marinated in pomegranate juice is famous in the San Francisco Bay Area from his days as a restaurant proprietor and popular caterer. Dennis Cakebread remembers that the first time he ever entertained at home, he prepared Narsai's lamb. Brian has adapted the recipe slightly, reducing the marinade to create a basting glaze that accentuates the sweet-sour flavor of pomegranate. The dish is elegant and foolproof, so even a novice cook can look like a pro. Allow at least six hours for the lamb to marinate.

2 cups pomegranate juice (from concentrate), preferably Pom Wonderful brand

1 yellow onion, coarsely chopped

3 cloves garlic

1 teaspoon minced fresh rosemary

2 teaspoons kosher salt

1/2 teaspoon freshly ground black pepper

2 eight-rib racks of lamb

In a blender or food processor, combine the pomegranate juice, onion, garlic, rosemary, salt, and pepper. Blend well. Put the lamb in a nonreactive container. Add the marinade and turn the lamb in the marinade to coat it on all sides. Cover and refrigerate for at least 6 hours or overnight.

Remove the lamb from the marinade and strain the marinade through a fine sieve into a small saucepan, pushing on the solids with a rubber spatula to extract as much liquid as possible. Simmer over high heat until reduced to 1/2 cup.

Preheat the oven to 450°F.

Set the meat on a rack in a baking sheet. Roast until the lamb registers 130°F (for medium) on an instant-read thermometer, about 30 minutes, basting every 10 minutes with the reduced marinade. Let rest for at least 10 minutes before carving into chops.

Enjoy with Cakebread Cellars Napa Valley Cabernet Sauvignon or another rich and firmly structured red wine.

Savoring Local Lamb

BRIAN BEGAN TO PURCHASE whole lambs for the winery when he met Don Watson and tasted his extraordinary Napa Valley lamb. Don only sells whole carcasses, so Brian had to master the butchery if he wanted the meat.

Don cleverly gets two revenue streams from his animals. He rents the sheep to vineyard owners as mobile and agile weed eaters. (He calls that business Wooly Weeders.) The young lambs graze at their mothers' sides on vineyard cover crops until they reach market weight, then they are sold to winery chefs and high-end restaurants. The milk-fed spring lamb we receive

from Don is so mild and tender that it makes converts of many winery guests who think they don't like lamb.

Don taught Brian how to break down the carcass, and Brian has developed uses for every part. Typically, he braises the shoulders and shanks; grills or roasts the loins, racks, and legs; grinds trim for meatballs or lamb "sliders"; and makes stock with the bony parts. Insuring that nothing useful gets thrown away is a gratifying culinary challenge. "I'm a better cook for it," says Brian.

Pancetta-Wrapped Pork Tenderloin with Tomato Fondue

SERVES 8

Our charcuterie supplier, Taylor Boetticher of Napa's Fatted Calf (opposite page), had the fine idea to wrap a pork tenderloin in a cloak of paper-thin pancetta. The pancetta bastes the lean tenderloin as it cooks, so the meat remains moist. A thyme-scented tomato fondue makes a light, summery accompaniment, suggested by 2009 Workshop participant Scott Gottlich. Add some sautéed Blue Lake beans or a slice of Mediterranean Summer Vegetable Gratin (page 158) to complete the plate.

You can roast only one tenderloin, if you like, but you may need to reduce the heat as you sear it because of the reduced volume of meat in the skillet. Do prepare the full amount of tomato fondue, however. You won't have enough volume for the blender otherwise, and you won't regret having extra. Note that the pork needs to marinate overnight.

30 paper-thin slices pancetta (further directions follow)

2 pork tenderloins (about 1 pound each)

Kosher salt and freshly ground black pepper

2 tablespoons Dijon mustard

1 tablespoon minced fresh thyme

TOMATO FONDUE

1 pound plum tomatoes, halved lengthwise

Kosher salt and freshly ground black pepper

1 1/2 teaspoons minced fresh thyme

6 tablespoons extra-virgin olive oil

3 cloves garlic, unpeeled

3 tablespoons unsalted butter

2 tablespoons extra-virgin olive oil

Ask your butcher or deli clerk to place 15 coiled pancetta slices on each of two sheets of deli paper, arranged in three rows of five slices each. The five slices should overlap slightly, and the rows should overlap slightly. The objective is to create two "beds" of sliced pancetta in which to wrap the tenderloins.

Trim the thin silvery membrane, or silverskin, and any external fat from each tenderloin. Season generously with salt and pepper on all sides. Brush mustard all over the tenderloins, then season with thyme.

Place a tenderloin on a bed of pancetta. With the aid of the deli paper, roll the loin to encase it in pancetta. Remove the paper. Repeat with the second tenderloin. Place the pancetta-wrapped tenderloins on a tray and cover with plastic wrap. Refrigerate overnight.

Preheat the oven to 350°F.

For the tomato fondue: Put the tomatoes, cut side up, on a baking sheet and season with salt and pepper. Sprinkle with thyme and drizzle with olive oil. Scatter the garlic cloves around the tomatoes. Bake until the tomatoes are tender, 30 to 35 minutes. When the tomatoes are cool enough to handle, discard the skins and seeds. Chop the tomatoes coarsely. Squeeze the softened garlic from the skins.

Combine the butter, tomatoes, and garlic in a medium saucepan over medium heat. Simmer, stirring, until the tomatoes collapse into a near puree, about 5 minutes. Puree in a blender. Return to the saucepan and keep warm over low heat.

continued on next page

Raise the oven temperature to 400°F. Heat a large ovenproof skillet over high heat. Add the 2 tablespoons olive oil. When the oil is hot, add the tenderloins and sear the pork all over, about 4 minutes total. Transfer the skillet to the oven and roast until the pork registers 140°F on an instant-read thermometer, about 20 minutes. Transfer the tenderloins to a cutting board and let rest for 5 minutes before carving.

Cut each loin into 8 medallions. Put 2 medallions on each dinner plate. Put a dollop of warm tomato fondue on top of the meat or alongside. Serve immediately.

Enjoy with Cakebread Cellars Anderson Valley Pinot Noir or another medium-bodied red wine.

Braised Radishes and Sugar Snap Peas

SERVES 4

Many people never think to cook radishes, but they are delicious when braised gently in butter. Brian likes to pair them with sugar snap peas, which mature in Dolores's garden at about the same time. You could add other spring vegetables, such as turnips, baby carrots, or English peas. Blanch them separately (as for the sugar snap peas here) so they don't pick up any radish color, then combine them all just long enough to reheat. Serve with Slow-Roasted King Salmon with Garden Herbs (page 110) or spring lamb.

1 pound sugar snap peas, ends trimmed, halved crosswise

4 tablespoons unsalted butter

3 dozen round red radishes, trimmed of greens and halved

Pinch of kosher salt

Pinch of sugar

1/2 cup vegetable stock (page 191) or water

Bring a medium pot of salted water to a boil over high heat. Add the peas and blanch just long enough to remove the raw taste, about 30 seconds. Drain and cool quickly in ice water, then drain again and pat dry.

Melt the butter in a medium saucepan over medium heat. Add the radishes, salt, and sugar. Stir to coat, then add the stock, cover, and simmer gently until tender when pierced, 7 to 8 minutes. Add the peas and cook, stirring, until they are hot. Taste for seasoning. Serve immediately.

Roasted Mushrooms and Baby Artichokes

SERVES 4

Brian sometimes roasts mushrooms and artichokes in the winery's pizza oven alongside a chicken, but the vegetables will color up beautifully in a hot home oven, too. Serve them, browned and sizzling, as an accompaniment to a roast or to Grilled Bone-In Ribeye Steak with Garlic Sauce (page 138). Or pair with polenta for a meatless meal.

12 baby artichokes (about 2 ounces each)

5 tablespoons extra-virgin olive oil

1 tablespoon freshly squeezed lemon juice

1 1/2 pounds mixed fresh mushrooms, such as large cremini, shiitake, trumpet, or oyster mushrooms

2 large cloves garlic, minced

2 teaspoons minced fresh thyme

Kosher salt and freshly ground black pepper

2 tablespoons chopped flat-leaf parsley

1/2 lemon

Preheat the oven to 400°F.

Peel back the outer leaves of the artichokes until they break off at the base. Keep removing leaves until you reach the pale green heart. Cut across the top of the heart to remove the pointed leaf tips. If the stem is still attached, cut it down to 1/2 inch, then trim the stem and base to remove any dark green or brown parts. Cut the artichokes in half lengthwise, then put them in a baking dish large enough to hold them and the mushrooms in a single layer. Add the olive oil and lemon juice and toss to coat.

Remove most the of the cremini stems and all of the tough shiitake stems. Remove the bottom inch or so of the trumpet mushrooms, which tends to be fibrous. Oyster mushrooms have more tender stems, so simply remove any browned ends. Slice the mushroom caps in half or into thirds. Cut the stems in half and then into pieces about the same size as the mushrooms.

Add the trimmed mushrooms and the garlic and thyme to the baking dish. Season with salt and pepper and toss well.

Cover the dish with foil and bake until the mushrooms have released some of their liquid and the juices are steaming, 20 to 30 minutes. Remove the foil and raise the oven temperature to 450°F. If you have a convection fan, turn it on. Continue roasting, stirring once or twice, until the artichokes are tender when pierced and both the mushrooms and the artichokes are well browned and beginning to caramelize in spots, 15 to 20 minutes. Stir in the chopped parsley. Taste for salt and pepper and add a squeeze of lemon juice. Serve hot.

Summer Bean Stew with Pancetta

SERVES 8 AS A MAIN DISH, 12 AS A SIDE DISH

With names like Good Mother Stallard, Goat's Eye, and Yellow Indian Woman, the dried heirloom beans from Rancho Gordo (see page 55) charm diners familiar with only generic dried beans. Rancho Gordo proprietor Steve Sando finds some of these intriguing beans in Mexico and Central America and arranges to buy them direct from the farmers. Others are grown on farms in Northern California.

You can use a single bean type for this dish, but Brian prefers to use multiple varieties, simmering them separately to accommodate their different cooking times. Just before serving, he unites them with a tomato sauce and some blanched fresh yellow and green beans. You could make a meal of this summer stew with a green salad and some crusty bread, or serve it as an accompaniment to grilled lamb. Note that the beans must soak overnight.

DRIED BEANS

1 pound dried heirloom beans, preferably mixed varieties

1½ yellow onions, peeled, cut into thick wedges

3 carrots, peeled, cut into large chunks

3 celery ribs, cut into large chunks

3 bay leaves

Kosher salt

¼ pound yellow wax beans, ends trimmed, cut into ½-inch pieces

¼ pound slender green beans, ends trimmed, cut into ½-inch pieces

2 tablespoons extra-virgin olive oil

¼ pound pancetta, diced

1 yellow onion, finely chopped

2 cloves garlic, minced

1½ cups peeled, seeded, and diced plum tomatoes (fresh or canned)

¼ cup chopped flat-leaf parsley

Freshly ground black pepper

For the dried beans: Keeping the beans separate by variety, soak them overnight in water to cover generously. Drain. Put each type in a separate saucepan and add cold water to cover by 3 inches.

Divide the onions, carrots, celery, and bay leaves among the pots. Bring to a boil over high heat, skimming any foam. Reduce the heat to maintain a bare simmer and cook, uncovered, until the beans are tender, about 1 hour or more, depending on age. Season to taste with salt and let cool in the broth. Drain the beans, reserving the broths separately. Discard the vegetables and bay leaves.

Bring a large pot of salted water to a boil over high heat. Add the wax and green beans together and cook until just tender, 3 to 5 minutes. Drain, transfer to ice water to chill, and drain again.

Heat the olive oil in a large, wide pot over high heat. Add the pancetta and sauté until it begins to crisp, 3 to 5 minutes. Add the onion and garlic, lower the heat to medium, and cook until the onion softens, about 5 minutes. Add the tomatoes and cook, stirring, until the tomatoes soften and begin to form a sauce, about 5 minutes. Add the drained heirloom beans and enough of the reserved broth to just cover them, 2 to 3 cups. (Use the most flavorful broth first, then supplement with the others if needed. Freeze any remaining broth for soup or risotto.) Bring to a simmer and cook gently for about 10 minutes to thicken the juices and blend the flavors. Stir in the yellow and green beans and the parsley. Simmer for about 2 minutes longer, then season with salt and pepper. Serve hot.

Enjoy with Cakebread Cellars Dancing Bear Ranch Cabernet Sauvignon or another robust red wine.

Blistered Cherry Tomatoes

SERVES 4

This five-minute side dish would complement any fish or meat from the grill, from swordfish to pork chops. Save the recipe for summer, when the cherry tomatoes have thin skins and you can find them in a rainbow of colors—red, gold, yellow, and green—at a farmers' market. Brian also spoons these juicy tomatoes over Grilled Bone-In Ribeye Steak with Garlic Sauce (page 138).

2 tablespoons extra-virgin olive oil

1 large shallot, minced

1 pound cherry tomatoes, preferably mixed colors

Kosher salt and freshly ground black pepper

2 tablespoons coarsely chopped flat-leaf parsley

1 teaspoon minced fresh thyme

1 teaspoon coarsely chopped fresh basil

Warm a large skillet over high heat. Add the olive oil and swirl to coat. Add the shallot and sauté for about 30 seconds to release some of its fragrance, then add the cherry tomatoes. Season to taste with salt and pepper. Add the parsley, thyme, and basil. Cook, stirring, until the tomato skins blister and split, 1 to 2 minutes depending on ripeness. Serve immediately.

Mediterranean Summer Vegetable Gratin

SERVES 8 TO 10

Adapted from a recipe from chef Gary Danko, who participated in the 1994 Workshop, this gratin relies on bread crumbs sprinkled between the vegetable layers to absorb the savory juices. After the gratin cools and settles, you can slice it like a cake and the layers will hold together. All the flavors that suggest a Provençal summer are gathered here—garlic and basil, tomato, fennel, and thyme. Serve the gratin with roast or grilled lamb or a store-bought spit-roasted chicken. Because it tastes best warm or at room temperature, you can bake it before dinner guests arrive.

7 tablespoons extra-virgin olive oil, plus more for the baking dish

3 yellow onions, halved and sliced

1 large fennel bulb, halved, cored, and sliced

2 cloves garlic, thinly sliced

2 sprigs fresh thyme

Kosher salt

1 globe eggplant, 1 1/4 to 1 1/2 pounds

1 pound zucchini

1 cup freshly grated Parmesan cheese

3/4 cup fine fresh bread crumbs

1/4 cup coarsely chopped fresh basil

1/4 cup finely chopped flat-leaf parsley

1/4 cup thinly sliced scallions, green parts only, or chives

1 tablespoon coarsely chopped fresh thyme

Freshly ground black pepper

1 1/2 pounds large tomatoes, sliced 1/4 inch thick

In a large, wide pot, heat 3 tablespoons of the olive oil over medium heat. Add the onions, fennel, garlic, thyme sprigs, and a pinch of salt. Cook until the vegetables are golden, soft, and sweet, about 30 minutes. Remove the thyme sprigs.

Trim the ends of the eggplant, peel it, and slice crosswise 1/4 to 1/3 inch thick. Trim the ends of the zucchini and slice on the diagonal as thickly as the eggplant.

Place the eggplant slices on a heavy baking sheet. Sprinkle both sides with salt, using a total of 1 tablespoon. Let rest for about 20 minutes to draw out moisture. With paper towels, blot the eggplant on both sides.

In a bowl, combine the cheese, bread crumbs, basil, parsley, scallions, chopped thyme, salt to taste, and several grinds of pepper. Mix well with your hands.

Preheat the oven to 400°F.

In a 16 by 10-inch oval gratin dish, or a shallow baking dish of similar capacity, spread the fennel-onion mixture in an even layer. Sprinkle with one-quarter of the bread crumb mixture. Top with half of the eggplant slices, overlapping them slightly, then with another quarter of the bread crumb mixture, the remaining eggplant slices, and another quarter of the bread crumb mixture. For the final layer, make overlapping rows of sliced zucchini and tomatoes, pressing them firmly into place. Season with salt and pepper. Top with the remaining bread crumb mixture. Drizzle with the remaining 4 tablespoons olive oil.

Bake the gratin for 1 hour, then remove from the oven, tilt the baking dish slightly and spoon some of the juices over the surface. Return to the oven until the gratin is nicely colored on top and the zucchini are tender but not mushy, about 10 minutes longer. The gratin is best when allowed to rest for at least 1 hour before serving. Serve warm or at room temperature.

Summer Vegetable Stew with Oregano and Chiles

SERVES 6

A spicy vegetable side dish from Chef Jon Mortimer, a 2007 Workshop participant, inspired this more substantial stew. By adding more summer vegetables, such as chayote and corn, Brian elevated Chef Mortimer's dish to entrée status. Prepared with vegetable stock, it is suitable for vegetarians.

2 tablespoons extra-virgin olive oil

1 large yellow onion, chopped

1 yellow bell pepper, seeded, cut into ½-inch dice

1 cup fresh corn kernels cut from the cob

1 poblano chile, seeded, cut into ½-inch dice

1 serrano chile, seeded and minced

2 cloves garlic, minced

1 teaspoon dried Mexican oregano

1 cup peeled, seeded, and diced plum tomatoes (fresh or canned)

3 cups chicken stock (page 190) or vegetable stock (page 191)

Kosher salt

2 chayotes, peeled, halved, pitted, and cut into ¾-inch dice

2 zucchini, ends removed, cut into ¾-inch dice

¼ cup chopped cilantro, plus more for garnish

Mexican-Style Green Rice (page 100)

6 lime wedges for serving

In a large pot, warm the olive oil over medium heat. Add the onion, bell pepper, corn, poblano and serrano chiles, garlic, and oregano. Sauté for about 5 minutes to soften the vegetables. Add the tomatoes and cook, stirring, for about 1 minute. Add the stock, season to taste with salt, and bring to a simmer. Add the chayotes and simmer gently for 15 minutes. Add the zucchini and simmer until the zucchini is just tender, about 10 minutes. Stir in the cilantro and taste for salt.

To serve, divide the rice among 6 shallow bowls and top with the stew. Garnish with more chopped cilantro and accompany each portion with a lime wedge.

Enjoy with Cakebread Cellars Sauvignon Blanc or another medium-bodied, crisp white wine.

Roasted Cauliflower with Toasted Bread Crumbs and *Gremolata*

SERVES 4

Most people steam or boil cauliflower, but roasting really brings out its sweetness. Brian tosses the sizzling cauliflower with *gremolata*, a mixture of parsley, garlic, and lemon zest—aromatic ingredients that release their aromas when they hit the hot vegetable. Toasted bread crumbs provide a pleasing crunch. Serve as an accompaniment to tuna or swordfish, or toss with spaghetti.

1 large cauliflower (about 2¹/₂ pounds)

3 tablespoons plus 2 teaspoons extra-virgin olive oil

Kosher salt and freshly ground black pepper

3 tablespoons coarse dry bread crumbs

2 tablespoons chopped flat-leaf parsley

2 tablespoons chopped capers

¹/₂ teaspoon grated lemon zest

1 clove garlic, minced

¹/₂ lemon

Preheat the oven to 450°F. Cut the cauliflower florets from the core, then cut the florets into bite-size pieces. Toss the cauliflower with the 3 tablespoons olive oil and season with salt and pepper. Place on a heavy baking sheet and roast until the florets are caramelized in spots and tender, about 20 minutes, turning the tray periodically and stirring the florets so they cook evenly.

Heat the remaining 2 teaspoons olive oil in a small skillet over high heat. Add the bread crumbs and a pinch of salt and cook, stirring constantly, until they are toasty and golden brown, about 1 minute. Remove from the heat and let cool.

In a small bowl, combine the parsley, capers, lemon zest, and garlic.

Put the hot cauliflower in a serving bowl and add the parsley mixture. Toss well. Add a squeeze of lemon juice and toss again. Sprinkle with the bread crumbs. Serve hot.

Braised Summer Vegetables with Basil Broth and Vella Cheese Crisps

SERVES 6

Like most of the chefs we take to visit Forni-Brown Gardens (see page 164) in Calistoga, Rocco di Spirito was overwhelmed by the bounty. This farm grows impeccable lettuces, tomatoes, herbs, and other produce for some of the most discriminating restaurants in Napa Valley. For his astonishing first course at the 2000 Workshop, Rocco used Forni-Brown beets, baby carrots, tiny tomatoes, and three kinds of basil. This aromatic stovetop braise is an adaptation of the more elaborate dish he made.

1 dozen golden or Chioggia beets, or a combination, golf ball size

BASIL BROTH

4 loosely packed cups fresh basil leaves

1 1/2 cups hot vegetable stock (page 191)

Kosher salt

CHEESE CRISPS

3/4 cup coarsely grated Vella Dry Jack cheese

18 baby carrots, peeled

1 cup vegetable stock (page 191)

1 tablespoon unsalted butter

1/2 pint cherry tomatoes

2 tablespoons thinly sliced fresh chives

1 tablespoon extra-virgin olive oil

Freshly squeezed lemon juice

Preheat the oven to 400°F. Roast the beets in a covered baking dish until they are tender when pierced, about 1 hour. Peel and quarter them and set aside.

For the basil broth: Bring a medium pot of water to a boil. Add the basil leaves and blanch for 10 seconds. Drain in a sieve or colander and cool quickly under cold running water. Squeeze as much liquid out of the leaves as you can. Chop roughly. In a blender, combine the chopped basil and 3/4 cup of the hot stock. Puree well, then add the remaining 3/4 cup stock and a pinch of salt and puree again. Strain though a fine sieve into a small saucepan.

For the cheese crisps: Preheat the oven to 375°F. Line a baking sheet with a silicone mat, or lightly brush a nonstick baking sheet with olive oil. Place a 3 1/2-inch pastry ring on the baking sheet and fill it with 2 tablespoons of the grated cheese, spreading the cheese evenly. Lift the ring and repeat until you have used all of the cheese; you should have enough cheese for 6 crisps. If you do not have a pastry ring, line a baking sheet with parchment paper and trace six 3 1/2-inch circles onto the parchment.

Bake until the cheese bubbles and turns golden and the butterfat begins to separate, 8 to 10 minutes, rotating the baking sheet halfway through. Don't let the cheese brown or the crisps will taste bitter. Working quickly, lift the cheese rounds with a metal spatula and drape them over a rolling pin. It's okay if they overlap slightly. Let cool, then remove.

Cut the carrots in half crosswise, slicing on the diagonal. Put the carrots in a medium saucepan. Add 3/4 cup of the stock, the butter, and a pinch of salt. Simmer uncovered over moderate heat

continued on next page

until the carrots are tender when pierced and about 3 tablespoons of liquid remain, about 8 minutes. Add the quartered beets and the remaining 1/4 cup stock and stir for about 2 minutes to warm the beets through. Add the tomatoes, raise the heat to high, and stir until their skins just begin to split; don't let the tomatoes collapse. Remove from the heat and stir in the chives and olive oil. Taste for salt. Add a squeeze of lemon to brighten the flavor.

Warm the basil broth gently; do not allow it to boil. Put 1/4 cup broth in each of 6 warm soup bowls. Divide the vegetables among the bowls. Top each serving with a cheese crisp.

Enjoy with Cakebread Cellars Sauvignon Blanc or another medium-bodied white wine with good acidity.

One Garden in Eden

VINEYARDS, NOT FARMS, define agriculture in Napa Valley. The wine grapes here are so valuable that it's rare to find people growing anything else. That's one reason why Calistoga's Forni-Brown Gardens is such a treasured resource. Many of Napa Valley's top restaurants get their heirloom tomatoes, lettuces, and herbs from Forni-Brown's four-acre farm.

Although the company is largely a wholesale supplier, it opens the doors to home gardeners annually for a spring plant sale. For many valley residents, an April visit to Forni-Brown is as immutable as paying income tax and a lot more fun.

Brian says that Lynn Brown knows more about tomatoes than anyone he has ever met. Sometimes, for the Workshop, Lynn will bring a range of heirloom tomatoes (the farm grows 30 to 50 varieties each year) and lead a tast-

ing for the chefs, who are often astonished at the gamut of aromas, acidity levels, shapes, and flavors. It's an exercise as stimulating as any wine tasting.

In spring, Dolores gets many of the tomato and herb seedlings for the winery garden from Forni-Brown. Local chefs appreciate that their custom assortment of leafy greens is picked that morning and dropped off that day. Since the greens aren't traveling far, Forni-Brown can grow particularly delicate, fragile varieties that put the coarser supermarket mesclun to shame. When we bring Workshop chefs to Forni-Brown for a visit, they are bowled over by the selection and freshness. By the time they leave the farm, they are mentally revising their course for that evening to include some favorite item from Forni-Brown.

Potato and Celery Root Gratin

SERVES 12

No one, no matter how calorie conscious, can pass up this luscious gratin. Winery chef Tom Sixsmith has perfected it, finding just the right proportion of potato to celery root and the ideal ratio of milk to cream. Serve with a grilled steak or a pork roast, or with a standing rib roast for a special occasion.

2 tablespoons unsalted butter, plus more for the baking dish

3 pounds russet potatoes, peeled

2 pounds (2 large) celery root, peeled

3 cloves garlic, minced

2 cups whole milk

2 cups heavy cream

1 tablespoon kosher salt

Freshly ground black pepper

Whole nutmeg or pinch of ground nutmeg

1/4 cup freshly grated Parmesan cheese

Preheat the oven to 375°F. Butter a 9 by 13-inch baking dish.

With a mandoline or other vegetable slicer, slice the potatoes and celery roots about 1/16 inch thick. Keep the two vegetables separate.

Warm the butter in a 6-quart pot over medium heat. Add the garlic and sauté until fragrant, about 1 minute. Add the milk and cream and bring to a simmer.

Add the celery roots and cook for about 3 minutes, then add the potatoes, salt, several grinds of black pepper, and a few gratings of nutmeg. Cook, stirring, until the liquid thickens, about 7 minutes. Stir in the cheese.

Transfer to the baking dish and spread evenly with a wooden spoon. Bake until the potatoes and celery root are tender when pierced and the top is lightly browned, about 40 minutes. Serve warm, not hot.

Baked Endive with Ham

SERVES 6

This classic of *la cuisine grandmère* did not come to Cakebread Cellars via anyone's French grandmother. We learned it from Rich Collins, who introduced endive to the United States when he began cultivating it commercially in California in the 1980s, as a young man barely out of college. Naturally, he calls his product California endive, not Belgian endive, and he has almost single-handedly built an American audience for this shapely chicory. We have watched Rich's company, California Vegetable Specialties, grow exponentially, and we use his flawless endives year round in hors d'oeuvres and salads. Make *endives au jambon*—braised endives wrapped with ham and baked in béchamel sauce—on a blustery winter night, and bring it straight to the table in its baking dish.

3½ tablespoons unsalted butter

12 large Belgian endives, root ends trimmed

1 tablespoon freshly squeezed lemon juice

Kosher salt

2 teaspoons sugar

12 thin slices smoked ham

2 cups whole milk

1 bay leaf

2 tablespoons all-purpose flour

1½ cups grated Gruyère cheese

Pinch of freshly grated nutmeg

Freshly ground white pepper

Melt 2 tablespoons of the butter in a 12-inch skillet over moderate heat. Add the endives; they will fit snugly side by side. Add 1 cup water and the lemon juice. Season with salt to taste and sprinkle with the sugar. Cover with a round of parchment paper to keep the endives bathed in steam. Bring to a boil over high heat, then cover and adjust the heat to maintain a gentle simmer. Cook for 25 to 30 minutes, then turn the endives with tongs, re-cover with the parchment, and continue cooking until you can insert a knife easily, about 20 minutes longer. Set aside until cool.

Gently squeeze each endive to remove excess moisture, then wrap each in a slice of ham. Place in a single layer in a 9 by 13-inch baking dish.

Preheat the oven to 375°F.

Put the milk and bay leaf in a small saucepan and bring to a boil over high heat; reduce the heat to low. In another small saucepan, melt the remaining 1½ tablespoons butter over low heat. Whisk in the flour and cook, stirring, for about 2 minutes to eliminate the raw flour taste. Slowly add the hot milk, whisking constantly. Simmer until smooth and slightly thickened. (It will be thin.) Remove from the heat. Stir in ½ cup of the cheese. Season with nutmeg and white pepper. Remove the bay leaf.

Pour the sauce evenly over the wrapped endives. Sprinkle the remaining 1 cup cheese on top. Bake until hot throughout and bubbly, about 25 minutes, then place the dish under a broiler and broil until the surface is lightly browned. Let rest for 15 minutes, then serve.

Enjoy with Cakebread Cellars Napa Valley Chardonnay or another white wine with lush texture.

Parsnip and Sharp Cheddar Soufflé

SERVES 6 AS A MAIN COURSE, 8 AS A FIRST COURSE

This crusty soufflé rises spectacularly in the oven and makes a grand entrance when you bring it to the table. The pureed parsnips add an intriguing nuttiness to this otherwise classic dish. Make it a first course at a dinner party or the main event at a more casual autumn or winter meal. Accompany it with lightly dressed butter lettuces, perhaps tossed with some sliced avocado and blood orange segments. The recipe is from Chef Michael Smith, who participated in the 2000 Workshop.

FOR THE BAKING DISH

1 tablespoon unsalted butter

1/4 cup fine dry bread crumbs or panko (packaged Japanese bread crumbs)

1 pound parsnips, peeled and halved crosswise, then halved lengthwise

2 1/2 cups water

2 teaspoons kosher salt

1 bay leaf

3 tablespoons unsalted butter

1/4 cup all-purpose flour

7 large egg yolks

1 1/2 cups grated aged white Cheddar

1 tablespoon chopped flat-leaf parsley

1 teaspoon chopped fresh thyme

1/4 teaspoon freshly ground white pepper

8 large egg whites

Butter the bottom and sides of a 2-quart soufflé dish. Coat evenly with the bread crumbs.

Slice the parsnips into 1/2-inch-wide pieces and put them in a 3-quart saucepan with the water, salt, and bay leaf. Bring to a simmer over moderate heat, reduce the heat to low, and simmer gently until the parsnips are tender, about 20 minutes. Strain, reserving the water but discarding the bay leaf. Puree the parsnips in a food processor. You should have about 1 1/2 cups puree.

Melt the butter in a 2-quart saucepan over moderate heat. Add the flour and whisk for 2 to 3 minutes to cook the flour; do not allow the mixture to brown. Whisk in 1 cup of the parsnip cooking liquid. Bring to a simmer and cook gently, whisking often and scraping the sides of the pan, for about 5 minutes. Whisk in the parsnip puree and simmer, whisking often, for 1 minute longer. Remove from the heat and whisk in the egg yolks, cheese, parsley, thyme, and pepper. Transfer to a large bowl. Put a piece of plastic wrap on top of the mixture to keep a skin from forming, and let cool to room temperature.

Preheat the oven to 400°F. Put a baking sheet in the bottom third of the oven to heat. With an electric stand mixer or handheld beaters, or by hand with a whisk, whip the egg whites and a pinch of kosher salt until the whites are stiff but not dry. Gently fold one-third of the beaten whites into the parsnip mixture to lighten it, then fold in the remaining whites. Transfer to the prepared soufflé dish. With the tip of a rubber spatula, trace a circle about 1/2 inch deep and 1 inch from the rim of the dish; this tracing will produce a top-hat effect when the soufflé rises.

Set the soufflé on the preheated baking sheet and bake for 10 minutes, then reduce the oven heat to 375°F and continue cooking until the soufflé is nicely browned on top, well risen, and firm to the touch, 45 to 50 minutes longer. Serve immediately.

Enjoy with Cakebread Cellars Chardonnay Reserve or another rich and silky white wine.

DESSERTS

SPRING

SUMMER

FALL

WINTER

Floating Islands with Strawberries and Caramel Sauce

SERVES 8

Alexis and Eric Koefoed operate Soul Food Farm (see page 173) in a rural area of Solano County, Napa's neighbor. The eggs from their pasture-raised chickens are so superior to conventional eggs that they inspired a cooking class at the winery. For the class dessert, Brian created this variation on floating island, a retro French dessert that deserves to come back into fashion. The "islands" are poached meringues that, in the original version, float on vanilla custard—a superb way to showcase first-rate eggs. The unusual caramel sauce flavored with Cakebread Cellars rosé is Brian's addition.

VANILLA CUSTARD

1 cup whole milk

1/2 vanilla bean

3 large egg yolks

2 tablespoons sugar

1 1/2 pints strawberries, cored and halved, or quartered if large

2 tablespoons sugar

CARAMEL SAUCE

1/2 cup sugar

1/4 cup water

1/4 cup Cakebread Cellars Vin de Porche Rosé

1 quart whole milk

1/2 cup sugar

1 large vanilla bean

MERINGUES

4 large egg whites

1/4 teaspoon freshly squeezed lemon juice

1/4 cup sugar

For the vanilla custard: Place the milk in a small saucepan. Scrape the seeds from the halved vanilla bean and add them to the milk along with the pod. Bring to a simmer over medium heat, then set aside to steep for 5 minutes.

In a small bowl, whisk together the egg yolks and sugar until the mixture is smooth, thick, and pale. Gradually whisk in half of the milk mixture to warm the yolks, then whisk in the remaining milk. Return the mixture to the saucepan and cook over medium heat, stirring constantly with a wooden spoon, until the custard thickens and coats the spoon, 1 to 2 minutes. Do not allow it to boil or it will curdle. Strain through a fine sieve into a bowl set in an ice-water bath, then refrigerate. You can make the custard up to 1 day ahead.

Toss the berries with the sugar and set aside for 30 minutes. Pour off and reserve the juices.

For the caramel sauce: In a small saucepan, heat the sugar and water over medium heat, swirling the pan until the sugar dissolves. Bring to a boil and cook until the syrup begins to turn a rich caramel color, about 5 minutes. Once it begins to change color, it darkens quickly, so remove the saucepan from the heat shortly *before* you think the caramel is done to allow for carry-over cooking. Off the heat, add the wine, which will cause the caramel to harden. (Be careful, as the mixture may splatter.) Return to medium heat and cook, stirring, until the caramel dissolves. Remove from the heat and let cool slightly, then stir in the reserved strawberry juices.

Heat the milk, sugar, and whole vanilla bean to a simmer in a wide, deep pan, then adjust the heat to maintain a bare simmer.

For the meringues: With electric handheld beaters or in a stand mixer on medium speed, whip the egg whites and lemon juice to

continued on next page

soft peaks. Raise the speed to high, add the sugar gradually, and beat to stiff peaks.

With a large soup spoon or serving spoon, scoop about one-eighth of the beaten egg white mixture and drop it onto the barely simmering milk, as if making a dumpling. Repeat with the remaining egg white mixture, taking care that the meringues do not touch. They will swell as they cook, so you may be able to cook only 4 meringues at one time. Cook for 1 minute, then carefully turn with a spoon and poach on the other side until the meringue feels set, 1 to 2 minutes longer.

While the meringues poach, put a generous 2 tablespoons of vanilla custard in each of 8 shallow soup bowls. Spoon the strawberries in the center, dividing them evenly, then top with a meringue and drizzle the meringue with warm caramel sauce. Serve immediately.

Eggs with Soul

IT'S COMMON IN PROFESSIONAL KITCHENS to source meat, fish, and produce with care but to be less finicky when it comes to staples like eggs and butter. Then you meet someone with superior eggs and realize what you've been missing.

Brian met Alexis Koefoed at the Napa farmers' market, where he has found many new purveyors over the years. She had pictures of the free-range chickens on her Soul Food Farm in nearby Vacaville, and it was clear that these birds got plenty of fresh air, exercise, and a varied diet. He took a dozen eggs home with him and noticed a difference immediately. The yolks were sunset-orange and sat up high in the center of the white, a sign of freshness.

Urged by Chez Panisse, the famed Berkeley restaurant, Alexis and her husband, Eric, began raising chickens for meat, too. Compared to supermarket poultry, Soul Food Farm birds really are exceptional. They roam the farm's organic pasture, mature slowly, and develop that deep, old-fashioned flavor missing in fast-growing, factory-raised birds. Brian made fried chicken with Soul Food Farm poultry for the Workshop's purveyor dinner one year, and it was as memorable as any Michelin three-star meal.

It's a pleasure to be able to source eggs from a local family that farms in a wholesome and humane way.

Rose Petal and Sparkling Wine Sorbet

SERVES 8

Napa spice merchant Shuli Madmone has introduced many fascinating seasonings to our kitchen, including the dried rose petals we use in this sorbet. His shop, Whole Spice (see page 126), is a playground for adventuresome cooks, and in recent years, he has brought a collection of exotic seasonings to the Workshop. We grind the dried rose petals fine with sugar, then use that fragrant mixture to sweeten a sparkling wine sorbet.

1½ cups dried rose petals (see Note)

1 cup plus 2 tablespoons sugar

3 tablespoons freshly squeezed lemon juice

3 cups cold water

2 cups chilled sparkling wine, preferably brut rosé or brut

Raspberries for garnish

In a food processor, puree the rose petals with the sugar until fine. Stir the lemon juice into the cold water. With the machine running, add the lemon water through the feed tube in a slow, steady stream. Strain the mixture through a fine sieve, pushing on the solids, then stir in 1 cup of the sparkling wine.

Churn in an ice-cream maker according to the manufacturer's instructions. Transfer the sorbet to a container, smooth the top, and place in the freezer until firm.

To serve, put 2 tablespoons (1 ounce) of sparkling wine in each of 8 goblets. Add a scoop or two of sorbet and garnish with a few raspberries.

NOTE: Look for dried rose petals at natural-food stores, Middle Eastern markets, or spice shops such as Whole Spice (see Ingredient Resources, page 193).

Balsamic Ice Cream with Fresh Cherry Sauce

SERVES 8

If you have never dreamed of putting vinegar in ice cream and can't imagine what it would taste like, don't summarily dismiss the idea. Balsamic vinegar, reduced to a syrup, gives ice cream a pale plum color and a caramel note. If you can't get fresh cherries, serve the ice cream with sugared strawberries or baked figs. Accompany with biscotti or another crisp cookie.

ICE CREAM

1 cup balsamic vinegar

1 pint whole milk

1/2 cup sugar

1 vanilla bean

1 pint heavy cream

CHERRY SAUCE

1 pound fresh cherries, pitted and halved

1/4 cup Cakebread Cellars Syrah or other red wine

1/2 vanilla bean

1 tablespoon sugar

Freshly squeezed lemon juice

For the ice cream: Put the vinegar in a small nonreactive saucepan and bring to a boil over high heat. Lower the heat to maintain a simmer and reduce to 1/4 cup, 5 to 10 minutes. Transfer to a bowl and chill in an ice bath.

In a small saucepan, combine the milk and sugar. Cut the vanilla bean in half lengthwise, scrape the seeds into the saucepan, then add the pod as well. Bring to a simmer over medium heat, stirring to dissolve the sugar. Stir in the cream, transfer to a bowl, and chill in an ice bath. Strain to remove the vanilla pod. Whisk in the chilled balsamic vinegar reduction. Churn in an ice-cream maker according to the manufacturer's instructions. Transfer to a freezer container and freeze for at least 1 hour, or until the ice cream is firm enough to scoop.

For the cherry sauce: In a medium saucepan, combine the cherries, wine, vanilla bean, and sugar. Bring to a simmer over medium heat, stirring, and cook until the alcohol evaporates and the cherries release some of their juice, about 5 minutes. Transfer to a bowl and let cool. Remove the vanilla bean. In a blender, puree half of the mixture and stir it back into the bowl. Add lemon juice to taste. Chill.

To serve, divide the ice cream among 8 compote dishes. Spoon cherry sauce over the ice cream and serve immediately.

Four-Cheese Cheesecake with Strawberry-Rhubarb Compote

SERVES 16

Compared to cheesecake made primarily with cream cheese, this rendition of the American classic is notably light. We make it with Cowgirl Creamery (opposite page) fromage blanc, which is lower in fat than cream cheese, plus ricotta and mascarpone to enhance the texture. A thin layer of Cowgirl Creamery crème fraîche blankets the top. The result is an easy, elegant, lemony dessert to serve in slender slices with a fruit accompaniment, such as sugared berries, a raspberry sauce, or the strawberry-rhubarb compote suggested here.

CRUST

1¼ cups graham cracker crumbs

3 tablespoons sugar

Pinch of kosher salt

4 tablespoons unsalted butter, melted

1 pound (2 cups) fromage blanc

½ pound (about 1 cup) whole-milk ricotta

½ pound mascarpone

1¼ cups sugar

4 large eggs

2 teaspoons vanilla extract

Grated zest of 1 lemon

2 tablespoons freshly squeezed lemon juice

½ cup crème fraîche

TOPPING

1 cup crème fraîche

2 tablespoons sugar

STRAWBERRY-RHUBARB COMPOTE

2 pints strawberries, cored and halved, or quartered if large

2 cups (4 small stalks) rhubarb, cut into ½-inch dice

⅔ cup sugar

Preheat the oven to 325°F.

For the crust: Pulse the graham cracker crumbs, sugar, and salt in a food processor. Add the butter and pulse again until blended. Transfer to a 9 by 3-inch springform pan and press the mixture into an even layer on the bottom. The cheesecake will be baked in a water bath, so to prevent seepage, wrap the pan in a sheet of foil large enough to come halfway up the sides.

In a stand mixer fitted with the paddle, or with handheld electric beaters, cream together the fromage blanc, ricotta, and mascarpone until smooth. Add the sugar, eggs, vanilla, lemon zest and juice, and crème fraîche and beat until well blended. Transfer to the pan and spread evenly.

Place the pan in a larger pan and add simmering water to come halfway up the sides. Bake until the cheesecake is set, with only a slight wobble in the center when you jiggle the pan, about 1 hour and 40 minutes. Remove the cheesecake from the water bath and transfer it to a cooling rack. Whisk together the crème fraîche and sugar, then spread the topping over the surface. Return the cheesecake to the oven for 10 minutes, setting the pan directly on the oven rack. Let cool on a rack, then refrigerate until chilled, at least 4 hours.

For the strawberry-rhubarb compote: Put the strawberries, rhubarb, and sugar in a nonreactive saucepan. Cover and cook over medium heat until the mixture comes to a boil and the fruit begins to collapse, about 5 minutes. Uncover and cook for another couple of minutes, stirring, to thicken the mixture slightly. Let cool, then refrigerate until chilled.

To serve, run a small, hot knife around the edge of the cheesecake, dipping the knife in hot water as needed to keep the cheesecake from sticking. Remove the sides of the pan. Cut the cheesecake into 16 wedges and accompany each portion with ¼ cup of the compote.

Edible Treasures from West Marin

THE "COWGIRLS" OF COWGIRL CREAMERY—
Sue Conley and Peg Smith—have participated in
the Workshop for many years. The organic cow's
milk cheeses they make in West Marin—among
them, Red Hawk, Pierce Point, and Mt. Tam—now
have a big fan club nationwide, but Sue and Peg
still make time to attend our little farmers' market
at the Workshop. We use many of their products
on cheese boards throughout the year.

Cowgirl Creamery's old-fashioned small-
curd cottage cheese is typically on the breakfast
table during the Workshop, along with Bellwether Farms yogurt, fresh berries, and Marshall's Farm honey. Given the direct connection
between all these foods and the local landscape,
it would be hard to imagine a more evocative
"taste of the place."

With their marketing company, Tomales Bay
Foods, Sue and Peg have devoted themselves to
supporting small artisan food producers, especially in their community of West Marin. They
don't view other cheesemakers as competitors
but as colleagues who can help raise the profile of West Marin and enhance viability for all.
That collaborative spirit is what the Workshop
is about, too, so it's particularly nice to get an
approving nod from the Cowgirls.

Peach Crisp with Crystallized Ginger and Pecans

SERVES 8

Florida chef Oliver Saucy, who attended the 1995 Workshop, tosses the peaches in his fruit crisp with crystallized ginger—a nice touch. Serve warm with a scoop of vanilla ice cream or a dollop of whipped cream. Tapioca flour thickens the peach juices without making them cloudy or imparting a floury taste. If you can't find it, purchase pearl tapioca and grind it fine in a spice mill or coffee grinder.

TOPPING

1 cup all-purpose flour

1/4 cup light brown sugar

1/4 cup granulated sugar

Pinch of kosher salt

1/2 cup chilled unsalted butter

1/2 cup chopped toasted pecans

3 1/2 pounds ripe peaches (7 to 10 peaches)

1/4 cup plus 2 tablespoons granulated sugar

1 tablespoon tapioca flour

1 tablespoon dark rum

1 tablespoon finely chopped crystallized ginger

Preheat the oven to 375°F.

For the topping: In a bowl, combine the flour, sugars, and salt and mix well. Cut in the butter with two knives or a pastry blender or work it in with your hands until the mixture forms coarse clumps. Add the pecans.

Cut an X in the rounded end of each peach. Blanch in boiling water for about 30 seconds, then transfer to ice water to chill quickly. Drain, and peel the peaches; the skin should peel back easily from the X. Cut the peaches into 1-inch-thick slices, then cut each slice in half crosswise.

In a bowl, combine the peaches, sugar, flour, rum, and ginger. Stir gently with a rubber spatula to blend.

Transfer the peaches to a 9 by 9 by 2-inch baking dish, spreading them evenly. Sprinkle with the topping. Set the pan on a baking sheet to catch any drips. Bake until the topping is browned and the juices are bubbling, 45 to 50 minutes. Let rest for at least 45 minutes before serving.

Blueberry Cornmeal Cake with Buttermilk Sabayon

SERVES 8

When you marry a pastry chef, you don't have to perfect your baking skills, says Ben Barker, who participated in the 1990 Workshop. That's why Chef Barker—whose wife, Karen, is a pastry authority—limits himself to simple "beach cottage desserts," like this cornmeal cake. It's a home-spun, old-fashioned dessert that you can adapt to any summer berries. The sabayon dresses it up for company. Don't be surprised by the unorthodox method—it really works.

4 tablespoons unsalted butter at room temperature, plus more for buttering the pan

3/4 pound fresh blueberries or blackberries

1 tablespoon freshly squeezed orange juice

1/2 teaspoon grated orange zest

1/4 teaspoon ground cinnamon

3/4 cup plus 2 tablespoons all-purpose flour

1/4 cup plus 2 tablespoons yellow cornmeal

1 1/2 teaspoons baking powder

1/2 teaspoon kosher salt

2/3 cup sugar

1/2 cup whole milk

1 cup boiling water

BUTTERMILK SABAYON

4 large egg yolks

1/4 cup sugar

3/4 cup buttermilk

1/2 cup heavy cream

1/4 teaspoon vanilla extract

Preheat the oven to 350°F. Butter a 9-inch deep-dish pie pan.

In a bowl, stir together the berries, orange juice, orange zest, and cinnamon. Spread the berry mixture evenly in the buttered pie pan.

In a bowl, whisk together the flour, cornmeal, baking powder, and salt.

In another bowl, with handheld electric beaters, beat the butter until smooth. Add the sugar gradually, beating until blended. By hand, stir in the dry ingredients; the mixture will be crumbly. Gradually stir in the milk. Dollop the batter over the berries, then use an offset spatula or knife to spread the batter in an even layer that covers the berries.

Put the pie plate on a rimmed baking sheet. Pour the boiling water evenly over the batter. Bake until the cake is firm to the touch and a toothpick inserted in the center comes out clean, 55 to 60 minutes. Let cool until just warm.

For the buttermilk sabayon: Combine the egg yolks, sugar, and buttermilk in the top of a double boiler or in a stainless steel bowl that fits over the top of a saucepan. Set over a saucepan of simmering water; the double boiler top or bowl should not touch the water. Whisk constantly by hand or with electric beaters until the mixture doubles in volume, thickens, and is hot to the touch, about 10 minutes. Cool the mixture in an ice bath.

Whip the cream and vanilla to firm peaks. Fold into the cooled egg mixture. Chill, covered, until ready to use.

Cut the warm cake into wedges and serve with a dollop of sabayon.

Chocolate for Wine Fans

LAUNCHED IN SAN FRANCISCO in 2005, TCHO is an innovative chocolate manufacturer whose founders think like winemakers. They don't market their dark chocolate based on cacao percentage. Instead, they focus on flavor and showcasing intrinsic qualities of the cacao bean, such as the fruity or nutty notes.

As TCHO's chocolate experts point out, the cacao percentage doesn't tell you much about a bar's quality or intensity because cocoa butter is included in the calculation. A chocolate bar with a high proportion of cocoa butter to cacao solids could still boast a high cacao percentage without having a rich chocolate flavor.

TCHO differentiates its four single-origin chocolate bars by flavor profile: chocolatey, citrusy, nutty, and fruity. These flavor tags encourage consumers to pay close attention to the aromatic qualities, just as wine enthusiasts do with wine.

Typically, we conclude meals at the winery with a cheese course, but when the occasion calls for it, we might make individual warm bittersweet chocolate cakes or a chocolate-salted caramel tart to accompany our Cabernet Sauvignon.

We use cocoa nibs, the unsweetened roasted cacao beans, more often than chocolate in our winery kitchen because the nibs have intriguing savory applications. Pounded fine, they add a deep roasted flavor to a spice rub for game. Some Workshop chefs have used them as a seasoning for Broken Arrow Ranch venison.

Ice Cream Sandwiches with Chocolate Almond Cake and Marcel's Caramel-Banana–Chocolate Chip Ice Cream

SERVES 10

Our homemade ice-cream sandwiches get raves when we serve them for lunch at the Workshop. We assemble them with cake instead of cookies to make them easier to eat. You can use any homemade or store-bought ice cream, but this caramel-banana–chocolate chip invention from pastry chef Marcel Desaulnier, who participated in the 1989 Workshop, is beyond delicious.

1 tablespoon melted butter, for brushing

CAKE

1³/4 cups sifted powdered sugar

6 tablespoons unsweetened cocoa powder

2 cups plus 2 tablespoons almond meal

12 large egg whites, at room temperature

Kosher salt

5 tablespoons granulated sugar

ICE CREAM

1 pound ripe bananas

1 cup plus 2 tablespoons granulated sugar

1/8 teaspoon freshly squeezed lemon juice

2 cups half-and-half

1 cup heavy cream

4 large egg yolks

1/2 cup chocolate chips or coarsely chopped bittersweet chocolate

For the cake: Preheat the oven to 350°F. Line a 12 by 17-inch rimmed baking sheet with parchment paper and brush the sides of the baking sheet with melted butter.

In a large bowl, sift together the powdered sugar and cocoa powder, then stir in the almond meal.

In an electric stand mixer or in a large bowl with handheld electric beaters, whip the egg whites until frothy, then add a pinch of salt. Whip the whites to soft peaks, then add the sugar gradually. Continue whipping until the peaks are firm yet glossy. Gently fold in one-third of the dry ingredients, then fold in the remainder.

Pour the batter onto the prepared baking sheet and spread evenly. Bake until the cake springs back when touched, 12 to 15 minutes. Let cool completely, then place the baking sheet in the freezer until the cake is cold.

For the ice cream: Peel the bananas and mash them roughly with a wooden spoon. Cover with plastic wrap, pressing the wrap directly against the mashed bananas, and set aside.

In a saucepan, combine 6 tablespoons of the sugar, the lemon juice, and 1/4 cup water. Cook over medium heat, swirling the pan until the sugar dissolves. Bring to a boil and cook until the syrup begins to turn a rich caramel color, about 3 minutes. Once it begins to change color, it darkens quickly, so watch carefully, swirling the pan so the caramel cooks evenly. Remove the pan from the heat and add the half-and-half and cream—carefully, as they will splatter. Stir in another 6 tablespoons sugar and return the pan to medium heat. Bring to a boil, stirring with a wooden spoon to dissolve the caramel.

In a large bowl, whisk together the egg yolks and the remaining 6 tablespoons sugar until thick and pale. Whisk in about 1 cup of the hot caramel mixture to warm the egg mixture, then pour the

continued on next page

combined mixture into the saucepan of caramel and cook, stirring, until it visibly thickens and reaches 178°F on an instant-read thermometer. Pour over the bananas and stir well. Chill quickly in an ice bath. When cold, stir in the chocolate chips.

Churn in an ice-cream maker according to the manufacturer's instructions. Transfer to a freezer container and freeze until the ice cream is firm enough to spread without melting.

Take the cake from the freezer. Put a sheet of parchment paper and a cooling rack on top, then invert the cake. Remove the baking sheet and top sheet of parchment, and cut the cake in half across the middle of the long side. Spread one half with ice cream, making an evenly thick layer. Invert the other half, including the parchment sheet under it, over the ice cream. Return the cake to the freezer for at least 2 hours.

To serve, take the cake from the freezer and remove the top sheet of parchment. With a serrated knife, trim the edges of the cake neatly. Cut the cake in half lengthwise, then cut each half into 5 triangles. Transfer the triangles to a serving platter, lifting them away from the bottom sheet of parchment. Serve immediately.

Honey and Almond *Semifreddo*

SERVES 8

An Italian *semifreddo* is a frozen mousse, lighter than ice cream and made without churning. You can vary it according to season, incorporating flavors from raspberry to pear to chestnut. We like to make it with chopped toasted almonds and Marshall's Farm wildflower honey, collected from hives in one of our vineyards. The result tastes like frozen nougat. Serve with a thin, crisp cookie.

3 large eggs, separated

1/4 cup dry sherry

3 tablespoons honey

2 tablespoons sugar

1 cup heavy cream

3/4 cup marcona almonds (see Notes, page 41), coarsely chopped

Combine the egg yolks, sherry, honey, and 1 tablespoon of the sugar in the top of a double boiler or in a large stainless steel bowl. Set over the bottom of the double boiler filled with a few inches of boiling water, making sure the bottom of the bowl does not touch the boiling water. With a whisk or handheld electric beaters, whisk the mixture over medium-high heat until it is pale, thick, and frothy, about 5 minutes; the mixture should form a ribbon when you lift the whisk. Remove from the heat and chill in an ice bath.

In a large bowl, whisk the heavy cream to soft peaks.

In another bowl, whisk the egg whites to soft peaks. Add the remaining 1 tablespoon sugar gradually and whisk to stiff peaks.

Gently fold the whipped cream into the cooled egg yolk mixture, then fold in the beaten egg whites and 1/2 cup of the almonds. Divide the mixture among eight 8-ounce coffee cups. Tap the cups on a work surface to settle the mixture, then smooth the tops with the back of a spoon. Sprinkle with the remaining chopped almonds. Freeze until firm, about 2 hours. Take out of the freezer 5 minutes before serving to soften slightly.

Chocolate Sea Salt Cookies

MAKES ABOUT 4¹/₂ DOZEN COOKIES

The chocolate cookies that Ritz-Carlton chef Rob Wilson made for the 2009 Workshop delivered two surprises: tiny nuggets of chopped dark chocolate and little bursts of fleur de sel, a coarse French salt extracted by hand from seawater. The salt, although unexpected, seemed to heighten the chocolate flavor. Chef Wilson used cake flour to make the cookies especially tender. He served them with Crème Fraîche Sorbet (page 186), but vanilla ice cream would complement them as well.

2 cups plus 2 tablespoons sifted cake flour

¹/₃ cup plus 1 tablespoon sifted unsweetened cocoa powder (not Dutch process)

1¹/₄ teaspoons fleur de sel

¹/₂ teaspoon baking soda

5 ounces (10 tablespoons) unsalted butter, softened

¹/₂ cup raw sugar

¹/₄ cup granulated sugar

1¹/₂ teaspoons vanilla extract

¹/₂ cup finely chopped dark chocolate (about 2¹/₂ ounces)

In a bowl, combine the cake flour, cocoa, fleur de sel, and baking soda. Whisk to blend.

In an electric stand mixer or with a handheld electric beater, cream together the butter, raw sugar, and granulated sugar on medium speed just until smooth. Do not overbeat; the mixture need not be fluffy. Beat in the vanilla, then reduce the mixer to low speed and add the dry ingredients. Mix on low until the dough comes together—it will be crumbly at first—then mix in the chopped chocolate. Divide the dough in half, then shape each half into a round, flattened disk.

Working with one disk at a time on a lightly floured surface, roll the dough into a 10-inch round, flouring as little as possible to prevent the dough from sticking. Cut out cookies with a 1³/₄-inch round cutter (or a cutter of another size, if you prefer). You can gather and re-roll the scraps once.

Transfer the cookies to baking sheets lined with parchment paper or a silicone baking mat. Refrigerate until chilled, about 1 hour.

Preheat the oven to 350°F. Bake the cookies until they look dry on top and are dry to the touch, about 15 minutes. Let cool completely on the baking sheet. The cookies will keep for up to 1 week in an airtight container.

Crème Fraîche Sorbet

Lighter than a custard-based ice cream, Chef Rob Wilson's sorbet makes a refreshing accompaniment to summer berries, grilled peaches, or baked fruit desserts. Or scoop the sorbet into compote dishes and accompany with his Chocolate Sea Salt Cookies (page 185).

1¹/₂ cups water

1 cup plus 2 tablespoons sugar

2 cups crème fraîche

4 teaspoons freshly squeezed lemon juice

Put the water and sugar in a small saucepan. Bring just to a simmer over high heat, stirring to dissolve the sugar. Let cool completely. Whisk in the crème fraîche and lemon juice. Chill thoroughly, then freeze in an ice-cream maker according to the manufacturer's instructions.

Chocolate-Praline Bread Pudding with Cinnamon Cream

SERVES 12

When an occasion calls for an indulgent dessert, Charlie Trotter's chocolate bread pudding should be on the short list. Chef Trotter makes bread pudding glamorous, enriching it with bittersweet chocolate and topping it with crunchy handmade praline. By any measure, it's a "wow" dessert.

PRALINE

1/2 cup granulated sugar

1/4 cup water

3/4 cup coarsely chopped toasted pecans

PUDDING

1 1/2 cups heavy cream

6 ounces bittersweet chocolate, coarsely chopped

1 1/2 cups whole milk

3 large eggs plus 3 large egg yolks

1/2 cup granulated sugar

Pinch of kosher salt

6 cups crustless day-old bread, in 1-inch cubes

CINNAMON CREAM

1 cup heavy cream

1 tablespoon plus 2 teaspoons confectioners' sugar

1/4 teaspoon ground cinnamon

For the praline: Lightly oil a baking sheet or line it with a silicone baking mat. Combine the sugar and water in a small saucepan and cook over moderate heat, stirring until the sugar dissolves. Continue cooking without stirring until the sugar syrup turns to dark caramel, 5 to 7 minutes, swirling the pan occasionally and gently so the caramel darkens evenly. Monitor the caramel closely during the final moments as it can quickly go from perfect to burnt. Work cautiously, as hot caramel can cause a nasty burn.

Stir in the pecans, then immediately pour the hot praline onto the prepared baking sheet in a thin, even layer. Let cool until hard, then break into small pieces.

For the pudding: Preheat the oven to 350°F. Lightly butter a 9-inch square pan.

In a small saucepan, heat the cream to a simmer. Remove from the heat and let stand for 5 minutes. Put half of the chopped chocolate in a large bowl and pour the hot cream over it. Whisk until smooth.

In a bowl, whisk together the milk, eggs and egg yolks, granulated sugar, and salt until well blended. Add to the melted chocolate mixture and whisk well.

Add the bread cubes and allow them to soak for about 30 minutes, pushing them down into the liquid occasionally. Fold in the remaining chopped chocolate. Transfer the mixture to the prepared pan, spreading it evenly. Sprinkle the praline over the surface. Place the pan in a larger roasting pan and add enough boiling water to come halfway up the sides of the smaller pan. Bake until the pudding is firm to the touch, about 45 minutes. Remove the smaller pan from the water bath and let the pudding cool for at least 30 minutes.

For the cream: In a bowl, with a whisk or electric beaters, whip together the cream, confectioners' sugar, and cinnamon to soft peaks.

To serve, cut the pudding into 12 pieces. Serve warm, accompanied by a dollop of cinnamon cream.

Grandmother's Soft Gingerbread Cake

SERVES 12 TO 16

Of all the sublime dishes that chef Nancy Oakes prepared during the 1997 Workshop, it is her warm gingerbread cake that has entrenched itself at Cakebread Cellars. The San Francisco chef says that the basic recipe is her grandmother's, although Chef Oakes sometimes dresses it up with a ginger syrup. Brian serves it often in the fall, sometimes with a scoop of honey ice cream or just a dollop of softly whipped cream. As dark as milk chocolate, this fabulous cake is moist, spicy, and not overly sweet. Don't worry if it sinks a bit in the center as it cools. Once it is cut, no one will notice.

2 cups unbleached all-purpose flour

2 teaspoons baking soda

1¼ teaspoons kosher salt

1 teaspoon ground cloves

1 teaspoon ground ginger

1 teaspoon ground cinnamon

1 cup sugar

1 cup dark molasses

1 cup vegetable oil

3 large eggs

1 cup boiling water

WHIPPED CREAM

1 cup heavy cream

2 teaspoons sugar

1/2 teaspoon vanilla extract

Freshly grated nutmeg for garnish (optional)

Preheat the oven to 350°F. Butter and lightly flour a 9-inch-round springform baking pan.

In a bowl, whisk together the flour, soda, salt, cloves, ginger, and cinnamon.

In a mixing bowl with electric beaters or by hand with a whisk, beat together the sugar, molasses, oil, and eggs until well blended and smooth, 1 to 2 minutes. Add the dry ingredients and mix just until blended, scraping the bowl once or twice. Add the boiling water and beat just until smooth. Don't overmix or the cake will be tough. The batter will be thin.

Pour the batter into the prepared pan and place on a baking sheet to catch any drips. Bake in the center of the oven until a toothpick inserted in the center comes out clean, 50 to 55 minutes. Let cool on a rack for at least 15 minutes before removing the pan sides.

For the whipped cream: In a mixing bowl with electric beaters or by hand with a whisk, whip together the cream, sugar, and vanilla to soft peaks.

To serve, cut the cake into 12 to 16 wedges. Transfer to dessert plates and put a dollop of whipped cream and a few sprinkles of nutmeg on top.

BASIC RECIPES

Cakebread Cellars Chicken Stock

MAKES ABOUT 2 QUARTS STOCK

We always keep chicken stock in the freezer because it is the foundation of so many of our soups, stews, and sauces. Making stock is an enjoyable project for a rainy day, and the results surpass anything you can buy. Homemade stock tastes fresh and lively compared to canned broth, which typically relies on dehydrated vegtables and seasonings. Brian doesn't salt his chicken stock but you can add salt to taste if you like.

6 pounds chicken backs or wings, or a combination

2 yellow onions, coarsely chopped

2 carrots, chopped

1 celery rib, chopped

4 cloves garlic, smashed

3 sprigs flat-leaf parsley

2 sprigs fresh thyme

1 bay leaf

4 black peppercorns

Place the chicken in a large stockpot. Cover with 3 quarts cold water and bring to a boil over high heat, skimming any foam. Add the onions, carrots, celery, garlic, parsley, thyme, bay leaf, and peppercorns. Return to a boil. Adjust the heat to maintain a bare simmer and cook, uncovered, until the flavor is rich and concentrated, 4 to 6 hours. Strain into a large bowl set in an ice-water bath. When chilled, transfer to airtight containers and refrigerate for up to 3 days or freeze for up to 2 months.

Cakebread Cellars Vegetable Stock

The olive oil is a nontraditional addition, but Brian believes that it keeps the stock from darkening. He salts it very lightly to avoid overseasoning the dish in which the stock is eventually used. Vegetable stock tastes best when freshly made, but you can freeze it.

3 large onions, peeled and coarsely chopped

3 carrots, peeled and coarsely chopped

1/2 fennel bulb, coarsely chopped

2 kohlrabies, peeled and coarsely chopped

4 turnips, peeled and coarsely chopped

2 large celery ribs, coarsely chopped

1 large leek, white and green part, coarsely chopped

4 quarts cold water

1/2 teaspoon kosher salt

3 tablespoons extra-virgin olive oil

Put all the ingredients in a large pot and bring to a boil over high heat. Adjust the heat to maintain a gentle simmer and cook until the vegetables are soft, 30 to 40 minutes. Let cool, then strain. Refrigerate for up to 3 days or freeze for up to 2 months.

Cakebread Cellars Fish Stock

MAKES ABOUT 3 QUARTS STOCK

Any fish market that fillets whole fish can provide fresh bones for your stock. Call ahead to reserve the bones as some markets put them in their own stock. When you have shrimp, lobster, or crab for dinner, freeze the shells for the next time you make fish stock. The stock tastes best when freshly made, but you can freeze it.

2 pounds fish bones (from white-fleshed fish only; no salmon or other oily fish)

3 tablespoons extra-virgin olive oil

2 small yellow onions, halved and sliced

1 celery rib, sliced

2 carrots, sliced

1/2 fennel bulb, sliced

1 cup Cakebread Cellars Sauvignon Blanc

1 sprig flat-leaf parsley

2 bay leaves

Rinse the fish bones well to remove any trace of blood.

Heat the olive oil in a large pot over moderately high heat. Add the onions, celery, carrots, and fennel. Sauté until the vegetables soften, about 5 minutes. Add the fish bones, wine, parsley, bay leaves, and 3 quarts cold water. Bring to a simmer over high heat, skimming any foam. Reduce the heat to maintain a gentle simmer and cook for 30 minutes. Strain. Chill the stock quickly in an ice-water bath. Refrigerate for up to 2 days or freeze for up to 2 months.

Preserved Lemons

MAKES 10 PRESERVED LEMONS

A staple of the Moroccan kitchen, preserved lemons have a tangy, fermented taste. For most recipes, the pulpy flesh is cut away and only the thick peel is used. Brian uses preserved lemons in a flavored butter for Grilled Mahimahi with Preserved Lemon Butter (page 113) and in Manila Clams, Arugula, and White Beans with Preserved Lemon Vinaigrette (page 54).

10 lemons

About 1 cup kosher salt

Pinch of red chile flakes

1 bay leaf

2¹/₂ cups strained freshly squeezed lemon juice, or more as needed

Scrub the lemons well and trim the ends. Quarter them lengthwise but stop short of slicing all the way through the bottom so that the four quarters remain connected.

Working with one lemon at a time, spread it open gently and sprinkle heavily with salt all over, using about 1¹/₂ tablespoons per lemon. Pack the salted lemons tightly in a clean 2-quart wide-mouth canning jar. Add the chile flakes and bay leaf. Fill the jar to the top with lemon juice; the juice must cover the lemons, so add more if necessary. Cover with the jar lid and screw band. Refrigerate. Shake the jar twice during the first week to redistribute the salt and seasonings, then shake once a week after that. The lemons will be ready to use after 1 month and will keep in the refrigerator indefinitely.

Cakebread Cellars Pizza Dough

MAKES ENOUGH DOUGH FOR FOUR 8-INCH PIZZAS

You can make this dough entirely with all-purpose flour, but using part durum flour produces a more satisfyingly chewy crust. Look for durum flour at natural foods stores and online (opposite page). Although many yeast-dough recipes call for proofing the yeast first, Brian doesn't bother, and the dough never fails to rise.

1¹/₄ cups unbleached all-purpose flour, plus more for kneading

1 cup durum flour

1 teaspoon active dry yeast

1 teaspoon kosher salt

1¹/₂ teaspoons extra-virgin olive oil

1 cup cool water (about 75°F), or more as needed

In a medium bowl, combine the all-purpose and durum flours, yeast, salt, and olive oil. Add the water and mix by hand with a wooden spoon or a dough scraper until the dough adheres and forms a ball. Transfer from the bowl to a lightly floured work surface and finish kneading by hand, using as little additional flour as possible, until the dough is smooth and elastic, about 5 minutes. Place in a lightly oiled bowl and cover with plastic wrap. Set aside in a warm place and allow to rise until doubled in volume, 1¹/₂ to 2 hours.

Punch the dough down and divide it into 4 equal pieces. Shape into balls and set on a floured baking sheet. Dust the tops with flour and cover the tray with plastic wrap. Let rest at room temperature for 30 minutes. Proceed with your chosen recipe.

INGREDIENT RESOURCES

Only a handful of the ingredients used in this book may be difficult to find. The following merchants can supply them.

For *fregola* (Sardinian pasta):
Market Hall Foods
www.markethallfoods.com
888-952-4005

For heirloom dried beans:
Rancho Gordo
www.ranchogordo.com
707-259-1935

For dried rose petals and other seasonings:
Whole Spice
www.wholespice.com
707-778-1750

For durum flour:
Giusto's
www.giustos.com
888-884-1940

For bottled piquillo peppers:
Spanish Table
www.spanishtable.com
505-986-0253

For Bellwether Farms cheeses:
www.bellwetherfarms.com
888-527-8606

For Broken Arrow Ranch wild game:
www.brokenarrowranch.com
800-962-4263

For Cowgirl Creamery cheeses:
www.cowgirlcreamery.com
415-663-9335

For Hog Island Oyster Company shellfish:
www.hogislandoysters.com
415-663-9218

For Marshall's Farm honey:
www.marshallshoney.com
707-556-8088

For Point Reyes Farmstead Cheese
Company cheeses:
www.pointreyescheese.com
800-591-6878

For TCHO chocolate:
www.tcho.com
415-981-0189

ACKNOWLEDGMENTS

We would like to acknowledge and express our gratitude to the many people who have contributed to the success of the American Harvest Workshop over the years. First and foremost: the visiting chefs, who bring their passion and love of cooking to our winery each year; and the amazing purveyors, close friends all, who have donated so much time and knowledge to this unique event. Thanks also to the Napa Valley Potters for sharing their craft with us; to Workshop co-founder Bill Shoaf, who shared Jack's vision of bringing hospitality people together to learn from each other; to Narsai David for his friendship and early support; to Michael Weiss for contributing his food-and-wine-pairing expertise to the Workshop every year; and to photographer and friend Terry McCarthy for capturing so many memorable Workshop moments.

We are also indebted to our hard-working hospitality staff, including resident chef Thomas Sixsmith, who assisted in testing recipes for the book and is responsible for the beautiful meals enjoyed by our winery guests; to Brenda Godinez for teaching us about the cooking of her native state of Michoacán; and to Marcy Snowe, our gardener, who supplies the winery kitchen with astonishing produce all year long. Thanks also to freelance pastry chef Jennifer Contreras, who helped in refining some of the dessert recipes in the book.

We are grateful to editor Julie Bennett and the team at Ten Speed Press for helping us realize our vision for this second Cakebread Cellars book. Working with Ten Speed was just as enjoyable the second time around. We thank food photographer Marshall Gordon and food stylist Dan Becker for helping to make these recipes look so appetizing, and we thank Janet Fletcher for telling the story of the American Harvest Workshop so well. As big fans of her writing, we feel fortunate to have been able to collaborate with her on this project.

INDEX

All photographs by Marshall Gordon, except as noted below. Photographs on pages 4 (right), 5, 7, 8 (top), 9, 15 (top left, bottom), 16, 21, 27, 51, 55, 126, 140, 177, 180, and 202 by Terrence McCarthy; page 133 by Steve Batz, Steven Edward Photography; page 144 by Chris Hughes; page 147 by Jim Reichardt; and page 173 by Bart Nagel.

Library of Congress Cataloging-in-Publication Data

Cakebread, Jack.
  The Cakebread Cellars American harvest cookbook : celebrating wine, food, and friends in the Napa Valley / Jack Cakebread and Dolores Cakebread and Brian Streeter ; with Janet Fletcher. — 1st ed.
     p. cm.
  Includes bibliographical references and index.
  Summary: "A collection of 100 recipes and wine pairings celebrating twenty-five years of the Cakebread Cellars American Harvest Workshop, a groundbreaking annual event that explores Napa Valley's vibrant food and wine culture" —Provided by publisher.
  1. Cooking, American—California style. 2. Food and wine pairing. 3. Wine and wine making—California—Napa Valley. 4. Cookbooks. I. Cakebread, Dolores. II. Streeter, Brian. III. Title.
  TX715.2.C34C3324 2011
    641.59794—dc22
                                        2010053848
ISBN 978-1-60774-013-1

Printed in China

Design by Betsy Stromberg
Food styling by Dan Becker
Food styling assistance by Emily Garland
Prop styling by Susan Neuer
Photography/production assistance by Dan Mitchell

10 9 8 7 6 5 4 3 2

First Edition

MEASUREMENT CONVERSION CHARTS

VOLUME

U.S.	Imperial	Metric
1 tablespoon	$1/2$ fl oz	15 ml
2 tablespoons	1 fl oz	30 ml
$1/4$ cup	2 fl oz	60 ml
$1/3$ cup	3 fl oz	90 ml
$1/2$ cup	4 fl oz	120 ml
$2/3$ cup	5 fl oz ($1/4$ pint)	150 ml
$3/4$ cup	6 fl oz	180 ml
1 cup	8 fl oz ($1/3$ pint)	240 ml
$1 1/4$ cups	10 fl oz ($1/2$ pint)	300 ml
2 cups (1 pint)	16 fl oz ($2/3$ pint)	480 ml
$2 1/2$ cups	20 fl oz (1 pint)	600 ml
1 quart	32 fl oz ($1 2/3$ pint)	1 l

TEMPERATURE

Fahrenheit	Celsius/Gas Mark
250°F	120°C/gas mark $1/2$
275°F	135°C/gas mark 1
300°F	150°C/gas mark 2
325°F	160°C/gas mark 3
350°F	180 or 175°C/gas mark 4
375°F	190°C/gas mark 5
400°F	200°C/gas mark 6
425°F	220°C/gas mark 7
450°F	230°C/gas mark 8
475°F	245°C/gas mark 9
500°F	260°C

LENGTH

Inch	Metric
$1/4$ inch	6 mm
$1/2$ inch	1.25 cm
$3/4$ inch	2 cm
1 inch	2.5 cm
6 inches ($1/2$ foot)	15 cm
12 inches (1 foot)	30 cm

WEIGHT

U.S./Imperial	Metric
$1/2$ oz	15 g
1 oz	30 g
2 oz	60 g
$1/4$ lb	115 g
$1/3$ lb	150 g
$1/2$ lb	225 g
$3/4$ lb	350 g
1 lb	450 g